Sacred Strides

WALKING IN THE
POWER AND **PRESENCE**
OF THE
HOLY SPIRIT

Xochitl Dixon

Our Daily Bread
Publishing®

Dedicated to the one true God—the Father, the Son, and the Holy Spirit—with love. Special thanks to those whom the Holy Spirit led to equip and encourage me to use writing and teaching as tools for ministry, especially Dr. Alan Dixon Sr., Barbara Pfahlert, Dr. Leroy Gainey, Pastor Robert Lawler, the Dinkins family (Steven, Joyce, and David), and my Our Daily Bread Ministries family.

Contents

Before We Begin   7
Introduction: God with Me   11

1. Recognizing Holy Ground   17
2. The First Step   23
3. Accepting New Life   29
4. Receiving and Relying on the Spirit   35
5. Always and Forever   41
6. Accurate Reflection   47
7. Ever-Present Everywhere   53
8. Cease and Submit   59
9. Enduring Hope   65
10. Commissioned to Love   70
11. Better Together   76
12. Forever Changing   82
13. Always at Home   89
14. Love Ever Flowing   94
15. Joy Is Now and Forever   99
16. Peace of Mine   104
17. Unfailing Fortitude   110

Contents

18. A Lifestyle of Service 116
19. Fueled by God's Goodness 121
20. Forever Faithful 127
21. God's Gentle Hands 132
22. Who's in Control? 137
23. So Worth Loving 142
24. Prepared to Fight 147
25. A Celebration Place 153
26. Everlasting Hope 159
27. Strength in Surrender 165
28. Worshiping Warrior 171
29. Freed! 177
30. Living for the King 183
31. Flourishing Fruit 189

Conclusion: Where Do I Go from Here? 197

Before We Begin

On January 14, 2022, I sat up in bed and winced as a sharp pain shot across my lower back. The severity of my situation hit me when my husband, Alan, called an ambulance.

I couldn't walk.

For the first few days in the hospital, I couldn't even sit up in bed without assistance.

I'd lived with elevated nerve pain and muscle spasms since 1992, after doctors misdiagnosed an injury to my spine. Over the years my pain increased but I'd always had mobility. Decades of overcompensation led to more damage to my spine and elevated pain levels in my upper thoracic back, shoulders, and neck. Finally in 2012, after one doctor cared enough to truly listen to me, I began a complicated healing journey. I've had multiple procedures, but still suffer from severe muscle spasms, sharp nerve pain in my spine, and debilitating headaches.

As I put my trust in God's plan and pace in that hospital room, thirty years after my original injury, I was living out the messages I'd shared in my first devotional, *Waiting for God: Trusting Him for the Answers to Every Prayer*. This time, however, I couldn't rely on my strength at all because I had none to offer. And it was hard!

But something happened during that first night alone in

the hospital, something God used to bring me here. So I'm grateful for the opportunity to invite you to journey with me through each chapter in *Sacred Strides*. I didn't intend these chapters to be academic arguments that explain the greatest mysteries of the Christian faith. I didn't select the illustrations to boast how God worked or is working in the lives of a group of super spiritual, perfect people of abounding faith. I don't know anyone who fits that description anyway.

I didn't think *Sacred Strides* could be a theological essay about the doctrine of the Trinity. I never planned on using Scripture to declare the Godhead in three equally divine persons—God the Father, who offers salvation through God the Son by the power of God the Holy Spirit. However, this is the doctrine of my faith.

Instead, in each chapter of *Sacred Strides*, I worship the one true God. I rejoice in the life-transforming love of God the Father. I revel in the saving grace of God the Son. And I relentlessly proclaim the Holy Spirit as He is revealed throughout Scripture, even when the writers did not mention Him by name.

As we step into God's Word, we'll ask the Holy Spirit to help us understand the Scriptures both in their original context and as they can be interpreted for life application today. Standing firm on God's Word, we'll declare a statement anchored in His unerring and unchanging truth. We'll prayerfully explore how God has worked and is working in the lives of the people He created and loves.

Then we'll *inhale*—take in, ponder, and believe—the words the Holy Spirit inspired, protected, and placed in our hands in the form of Scripture. We'll *exhale* prayers and praises as we worship God by calling on the too-often-neglected name of the Holy Spirit. We'll invite the Spirit to help us trust what the Bible says is relevant and marked by His authority. We'll invite Him to transform us and empower us to take sacred strides of loving obedience on the holy ground of His constant presence. We'll pray God uses each chapter in *Sacred Strides* to reveal Himself more intimately as we surrender to Him more completely.

As our ever-present God continues His work in our lives, let's begin our journey with one of the most powerful and necessary prayers uttered this side of eternity:

Holy Spirit, I'm ready. I am willing. Do what You will!

Introduction
God with Me

STEP INTO GOD'S WORD
Ephesians 1:1–14

STAND ON GOD'S TRUTH
The Holy Spirit is God with us.

I thought I knew what it felt like to fully depend on God until the moment when I lost my ability to walk. I prayed silently as the paramedics strapped me to a special chair and transported me down the thirty-nine stairs from our third-floor apartment. After they transitioned me onto a gurney and lifted me into the ambulance, the EMT took my blood pressure.

He told me he didn't like my numbers and asked me to breathe slowly.

I inhaled, counted to three, then exhaled.

As I inhaled again, a sudden wave of peace flowed through me. When I exhaled, I knew God was with me.

The EMT smiled and said I was going to be okay. I closed my eyes and began saying silent breath-prayers.

I inhaled the God-breathed words of Scripture, which I had tucked into my heart as I read the Bible daily since 2001. I exhaled prayers and praises based on His truth. Through this practice, God shifted my attention away from my pain and toward His presence, His promises, and His people.

After the EMT updated the ER nurse and said goodbye, I prayed silently for their team. My husband, who was suffering from a torn Achilles, hobbled into the room on crutches. I prayed for him as he settled into a chair. Hours later, I prayed for the doctor who examined me, admitted me into the hospital, and encouraged Alan to go home and rest.

I prayed throughout the intake process. During my first night alone in that hospital room, however, worry and fear overwhelmed me. Once the nurse turned the lights off, I couldn't remember any Bible verses to inhale. I couldn't even think of the right words to pray as the woman in the next room wailed, begging doctors for relief. I inhaled as I sobbed for my neighbor. I exhaled, asking God to help her. Surprised when Psalm 46:1 popped into my mind, I inhaled: "God is our refuge and strength, an ever-present help in trouble." I exhaled and whispered, "Ever present. Always. Even here."

I continued breathing prayers. I can't explain how I remembered Bible verses I hadn't memorized. I don't know how to describe the depth of peace that poured over and around and into every crevice of my being. And I don't know how or when I fell asleep. But I do know that when the morning nurses arrived, I was still flat on my back in excruciating pain and still unable to walk. As I greeted everyone with a smile and encouraging words, I prayed for them silently. I felt God holding me, comforting me, being my refuge and strength.

Throughout the day I inhaled the biblical truths of Scripture that God the Spirit brought to my mind. I exhaled prayers and praises in the name of God the Son. I rested in the love of God the Father. I asked my husband to bring my Bible, my copy of the current *Our Daily Bread* devotional, and the boxes of my books that I had ordered for a big event we canceled during the pandemic. While in the hospital, I prayed for and with the people God sent to help me. I also handed out *Our Daily Bread* quarterly booklets and copies of *Waiting for God*, *God Hears Her*, and my children's book *Different Like Me*. Though I couldn't walk, the Holy Spirit enabled me to fulfill the Great Commission (Matthew 28:16–20) while living out the Greatest Commandment (Matthew 22:34–40) from my hospital bed. Something in me changed as my perspective shifted while I prayed and served others on that mission field. Before doctors released me, I wrote the first chapter of this book. To God be the glory, the honor, and the praise!

After returning home, I explored how the Holy Spirit worked in and through the lives of God's people in the Old and New Testaments, differently and powerfully. I rejoiced as I acknowledged the Holy Spirit—the third person of the Godhead. I praised Him for being as present today as He was before the creation of the world and throughout the sixty-six books of the Bible. I experienced peace and exhilarating hope in knowing that God connected His people in the Old Testament to the believers Paul ministered to in the New Testament era . . . to His people today . . . to me . . . and to you.

In Ephesians 1, Paul referred to the believers as "God's holy people . . . the faithful in Christ Jesus" (v. 1), those set apart and given intimate access to God the Father. He proclaimed this unearnable privilege as accessible only through the sacrificial offering of the Lamb—Jesus, God the Son—and possible only through the power of God the Spirit. Paul said that God has "blessed us in the heavenly realms with every spiritual blessing in Christ" (v. 3). He emphasized eternal blessings that are spiritual and soul satisfying, not temporal things that cannot last. Paul affirmed that those blessings flow through the closeness of God. Since God remains with us, it is the Christian's responsibility to abide in Him through faithfulness *in* Christ, not just *to* Christ. Paul said that God chose us in Him "before the creation of the world to be holy and blameless in his sight" (v. 4). He "predestined us," in advance and "in love," so He could adopt us into His family (v. 5). This personal relationship demands an awareness and acceptance of God as the initiator, builder, and sustainer of our faith. Paul's words lead us away from self-sufficiency and works-based theology. He points toward an all-encompassing trust in our all-sufficient God, which requires total reliance on and surrender to the Holy Spirit.

The moment we heard and *received* the gospel as truth— that millisecond when we crossed from unbelief to belief, into faith *in* Jesus not just as our Savior but also as our Lord—we were "marked in him with a seal, the promised Holy Spirit" (v. 13). The Spirit is He "who is a deposit guaranteeing our inheritance until the redemption of those who are God's possession—to the praise of his glory" (v. 14). He is the promise of our freedom from sin, the proof of salvation through Christ, the guarantor of our eternal inheritance, and the transformer of our hearts and minds.

In response to this gift, we are expected and empowered to live in Christ, through Christ, with Christ, and for Christ. We're not designed to live for God out of obligation or in our own might. Instead, from the limitless well of Christ's love, the Spirit enables us to love God and others. Our gratitude becomes an act of worship displayed through our obedience, service, and faith. However, we can do nothing without Him. So He requires us to call on Him, to pray. He won't just give us strength, peace, or hope—He *becomes* our strength, peace, hope, and even joy no matter what happens.

Believers in whom the Holy Spirit dwells stand on the solid ground of God's unchanging truth revealed in the Old and New Testaments. However, in every moment God has ordained for us on this side of eternity, we are also standing on the *holy* ground of His constant presence. When we feel physically, emotionally, mentally, or spiritually depleted, we can rejoice in the fullness of God the Father and worship God the Son by embracing our dependence on God the Spirit. If we can't *feel* God's presence, we can still pray confidently with the psalmist David: "The LORD is my shepherd, I lack nothing. He makes me lie down in green pastures, he leads me beside quiet waters, he refreshes my soul. He guides me along the right paths for his name's sake. Even though I walk through the darkest valley, I will fear no evil, for you *are* with me; your rod and your staff, they comfort me" (Psalm 23:1–4, emphasis mine). Jesus is Emmanuel, God with us. He gave us the Holy Spirit after He rose and ascended to heaven to be at the right hand of God the Father until He comes again—the second coming—as promised. So we can ask the Holy Spirit to heighten our awareness of His presence. We can ask Him to help us acknowledge Him with every breath we inhale and every prayer we exhale. And we can invite Him to empower us to rely on Him with every sacred stride we take.

Inhale

It's in Christ that you, once you heard the truth and believed it (this Message of your salvation), found yourselves home free—signed, sealed, and delivered by the Holy Spirit. This down payment from God is the first installment on what's coming, a reminder that we'll get everything God has planned for us, a praising and glorious life. (Ephesians 1:13–14 MSG)

Exhale

Holy Spirit, thanks for assuring us that You—the third person of the Trinity—are fully God and forever with us. Help us get to know You through the ways You've worked in and through the lives of Your people in the Bible, in our world, and in our lives. Help us acknowledge Your holiness and the holy ground we stand on because of Your constant presence. Empower us to honor that sacred space as we live in victory on this side of eternity until the day the Father calls us home or the day the Son, Jesus Christ our Lord, comes again. In Jesus's name, amen.

SACRED STRIDE

Ask the Holy Spirit to help you embrace the mystery and complexity of the Godhead and trust that He is the third person of the Trinity—fully and completely God—as He reveals His presence in Scripture and throughout each day of your life.

1

Recognizing Holy Ground

STEP INTO GOD'S WORD
Exodus 3:1–14

STAND ON GOD'S TRUTH
Believers in Jesus are always on holy ground
because the Holy Spirit is always with us.

I n 2019, a year after our move to Wisconsin from California, I connected with a Christian doctor. As he and his wife, Patty, prayed for me, God led him to a new medication to treat the constant sharp nerve pain in my spine that caused the spasms in my upper thoracic back. After the initial infusion, I stood without hunching over. I breathed without agonizing nerve pain for the first time since my injury in 1992. I wept as I thanked my doctor and his staff. I thanked God for sending me to the Midwest to meet my praying doctor.

Then the COVID-19 pandemic hit and shoved us into lockdown. I walked more, thanks to that new medication and Callie, my service dog trained through Tails for Life. Wearing a mask and respecting the social distancing rules, I met my neighbors. I enjoyed visiting ReachOut & Solid Grounds Coffee Shoppe, a small but mighty house of ministry that doubled as a Christian bookstore.

I served God, praised God, and prayerfully studied the Bible. I trusted the Scriptures and believed everything I prayed, said, and wrote to encourage others. But as I trudged through the months, the extreme weather, the isolation, and the divisions caused by racial tension and political discourse wore me down. I wrestled with discontent while missing our family and friends on the West Coast. Peace, hope, and confidence slipped out of my grasp. Physically, emotionally, mentally, and spiritually exhausted, I battled depression and loneliness. Then I began battling my husband. As the lockdown continued, we stumbled into each other's personal space and grew further apart.

I cried out to God: Why do I feel so empty and alone? I'm doing all I can.

As I grappled with my human analysis of the problem, the Holy Spirit nudged me to read Scripture and pray on social media. I showed up for my Pause for Prayer videos each day feeling weak and weary. God filled my dehydrated spirit with the revitalizing hope of His truth and love. However, wading through those months of despair led to a terrifying revelation: in serving God consistently, I had been slowly severing my personal *connection* with Him.

By relying on my own abilities, I failed to access the Holy Spirit's power in me. I knew the Holy Spirit is the Spirit of God who indwells all believers in Jesus. But knowing the truth wasn't the same as living in light of that truth. Intentionally or unintentionally, I had shoved the Holy Spirit to the sidelines and depended on myself.

Afraid to take matters into my own hands again, I asked God

to help me. I expected my journey to start in the beginning of creation, where Scripture first mentions the Holy Spirit as "hovering over the waters" in Genesis 1:1–2. But as I paused long enough to listen, the Holy Spirit led me to Midian, the place Moses settled after fleeing Egypt.

One ordinary day, Moses led a flock of sheep to the "mountain of God" (Exodus 3:1). In an ordinary place, "the angel of the LORD appeared to [Moses] in flames of fire from within a bush" (v. 2). As if the "strange sight" Moses saw was not extraordinary, Moses approached the burning bush in an ordinary way (v. 3). God called Moses by name twice, an unordinary act that signified God was about to move in an extraordinary way.

Moses's response, "Here I am" (v. 4), and his story before becoming a grown runaway, suggest a preexisting connection between himself and God. Hebrews 11:23 states that his parents hid him "by faith." Pharaoh's daughter, upon discovering him in a basket among the reeds of the Nile, rescued him and commissioned his biological mother to nurse him (Exodus 2:5–10). Moses's faith-filled parents probably had him around seven years before surrendering him for adoption to Pharaoh's daughter. During that time, they likely taught him to fear God.

This may be why Moses seemed ready to respond many years later when God called him. However, God stopped him from stepping into the sacred space of His intimate presence. "'Do not come any closer,' God said. 'Take off your sandals, for the place where you are standing is holy ground'" (Exodus 3:5).

God affirmed His holiness and the need for reverence. He assured Moses that He had seen all His people had endured. Then He sent Moses on a mission (vv. 7–10). But Moses responded, "Who am I that I should go to Pharaoh and bring the Israelites out of Egypt?" (v. 11).

By focusing on his limitations instead of the limitless power of the one true God who sent him, Moses doubted God. He could have asked, "Who is sending me and promising to walk with me? Who is this who has the power to communicate through a burning bush that is not even singed by the flames? Who is this who sees me, knows my name, and still chooses to use fearful and fallible me?"

God didn't address Moses's insecurities, though. He simply made another promise: "This *will be* the sign to you that *it is I* who have *sent* you: *When* you have brought the people out of Egypt, *you will* worship God on this mountain" (v. 12, emphasis mine). Even with this guarantee from the Lord Almighty, Moses focused on himself (v. 13). But God continued declaring His own identity. He said, "I AM WHO I AM. This is what you are to say to the Israelites: 'I AM has sent me to you'" (v. 14).

By questioning our abilities to go wherever God sends us, even when our obstacles and limitations are real, we're failing to rely on God with us and in us. We pray for help as if we're not sure God will deliver, instead of praying with confidence in all He's already promised and given through the Spirit. This mentality leaves us susceptible to severing our intimacy with God and diminishing our reverence of God without even realizing we're doing so.

God is not in the habit of sending His children on missions as loners. The Old and New Testaments declare God's power and constant presence with His people repeatedly. As Christ followers who have received the Holy Spirit, we spend every moment of every ordinary day *with* our extraordinary God. Everywhere we go is holy ground because the Holy Spirit is God with us. Every step we take with God will be on holy ground because of His ever-present existence and unsurpassable power.

The first vital step toward walking by faith in His power is acknowledging who the Holy Spirit is and always will be. We can feel confident in referring to the Spirit of God as *He*, not *It*, because His personhood is affirmed throughout Scripture. Jesus Himself introduced the Holy Spirit to the disciples in this way: "When the Advocate comes, whom I will send to you from the Father—the Spirit of truth who goes out from the Father—he will testify about me" (John 15:26). Jesus's words show that He and the Father and the Spirit—all equally and completely God—are one God in three divine persons who interact and communicate within the Godhead as well as with those who trust in Christ.

In John 16:8, Jesus said this about the Holy Spirit: "When he comes, he will prove the world wrong about sin and righteousness and judgment." The apostle Paul says the Spirit empowers us to understand and obey the Scriptures (1 Corinthians 2:9–16). The Spirit of God knows what we ought to pray for and intercedes for us in prayer (Romans 8:26–27). And these are only a few of the Spirit's qualities revealed through Scripture that reflect who He is and how He operates.

When we embrace the fullness of the Holy Spirit's personhood—He who helps, teaches, guides, comforts, feels, and loves—we are recognizing His wholeness and His holiness. By depending on and submitting to Him, we honor His authority as God. Knowing *He* will be our peace, our refuge, and our sustainer, we no longer cling to idols that fail to do what only God can do. We can approach ordinary days with extraordinary faith and take each sacred stride in the surety of God's never-ending presence and power.

Inhale

"Do not come any closer," God said. "Take off your sandals, for the place where you are standing is holy ground." (Exodus 3:5)

Exhale

Ever-present Spirit of God, thanks for being You. Forgive us for focusing on ourselves, whether we're shrinking back with insecurities, trying to grow in self-confidence, or excelling at self-help and self-assurance. Turn our eyes away from our limitations so we can be fully dependent on Your limitless might. Please continue fueling our faith with the knowledge of and confidence in Your identity and Your promises as we walk on the holy ground that affirms Your holy presence. In Jesus's name, amen.

SACRED STRIDE

Ask the Holy Spirit to reveal His presence, His holiness, His unchanging character, and His work, throughout Scripture, in your life, and in and through the lives of those around you.

The First Step

STEP INTO GOD'S WORD
Psalm 143:1–12

STAND ON GOD'S TRUTH
*The Holy Spirit empowers us to walk
in loving obedience and faith.*

I opened my laptop, steaming as I tapped my topic into the search bar—"local divorce lawyers." Months into the pandemic, I bowed under the mounting stresses of living without the comfort of our support network while adjusting to the freezing days in the tundra (aka Wisconsin). I couldn't stand feeling lonely when my husband was in the same room. I griped about everything he said and did. I snapped at him and became defensive. I blamed him for my unhappiness and did my best to make him unhappy. I believed he was doing the same.

Willingly wrestling with the Holy Spirit, I lived in attack mode. I flung flaming arrows of accusations toward the man I'd once vowed to love and cherish. I could not, would not see past my husband's faults as I remained strategically blind to my own. As a warring wife, I insisted my husband's sinful actions caused my sinful responses. If he didn't do this or that, I wouldn't have done that or this. Every time I prayed for our marriage and considered submitting to the Spirit, the Enemy reminded me that my husband hadn't admitted his wrongs or apologized.

Though I knew the true war wasn't against my husband, I had grown comfortable with putting him on the judgment seat. So when the Holy Spirit brought up Psalm 143, I thought God was comforting me. "LORD, hear my prayer, listen to my cry for mercy; in your faithfulness and righteousness come to my relief" (Psalm 143:1). Hallelujah! God knew I was right too. In joyful self-righteousness I began reading the second verse: "Do not bring your servant into judgment, for no one living is righteous before you" (v. 2).

I read David's descriptions of the pursuing enemy and related to his complaint: "So my spirit grows faint within me; my heart within me is dismayed" (v. 4). As I prayed, I rattled off the list of my spouse's offenses. Surely God would find him guiltier than me. But digging deeper into Scripture, I couldn't deny the truth. My greatest enemy was the devil, not any person God made in His image.

Acknowledging spiritual warfare reminded me that I needed to fight in the spiritual realm. This war strategy required me to step aside and call on the Holy Spirit to fight on my behalf *and* on my husband's behalf. I needed God's help to start praying for my marriage, which demanded I treat my husband as my ally, not my enemy. I knew these things before, so how did I become a warring wife? I found a hint in David's lament: "I remember the days of long ago; I meditate on all your works and consider what your hands have done" (v. 5). Neglecting the nurturing of my intimate moments of *connection* with God

24

made me easy prey for that prowling liar, Satan, who longs to destroy God's people and their relationships with God and others, especially Christ-centered marriages.

How long had it been since I rested in the stillness to remember all God had done in and through my life, my husband's life, and our marriage? I used to say we were on the brink of divorce from the moment we said, "I do." However, I didn't know Jesus then, and my husband wasn't walking with Jesus. We almost annulled our marriage during our honeymoon. We had grown accustomed to fighting, each blaming the other for our own failings and sinful choices. We drew lines in the sand and built concrete walls around our hearts so we wouldn't get hurt anymore. Over time, we learned how to dig under those walls to inflict deeper wounds with words that scarred each other's souls. Still, in His awesome goodness, God rescued both of us. He began working on saving our marriage after a three-month separation.

I surrendered my life to Jesus in 2001. My husband recommitted his life to Jesus in 2003. Our pastor baptized us with our son Xavier that year. Two years later my stepson also committed his life to Jesus. Though life did not instantly improve, my husband and I soon longed for our family to draw closer to Jesus. We followed a schedule to read through the Bible in a year with our sons, multiple times. We went to church together. We served the Lord together. We talked about the Bible, memorized the Bible, and taught the Bible together. My husband and I declared that everyone in our house would serve the Lord, and we led by example . . . except when we didn't.

And in Wisconsin we definitely did not.

Every time I became tempted to give up on our marriage, the Holy Spirit reminded me of how much He had transformed us as individuals and as a couple. And I couldn't deny that He still had lots of work to do in each of us and in our marriage. So that day, with tears streaming down my cheeks, I closed my laptop. I asked for forgiveness and texted my husband an apology. Alan didn't apologize to me at that time. So, sooner than I'd like to admit, the anger returned. I couldn't save my marriage. Neither could my husband. We needed spiritual intervention. As believers in Jesus, we both had access to the power of the Holy Spirit in us. But I couldn't control what my husband did. I could only control my willingness to submit to the Spirit's authority. It didn't matter what my husband was doing. I was only responsible for my actions, my readiness to submit to the Spirit and surrender to His guidance. In that moment, however, I wasn't living as if the Holy Spirit was my strength and peace. I wasn't living as if Jesus was my Lord.

I chose to sin.

Overwhelmed with that in-my-face truth, I asked the Holy Spirit to change me and help me to stop telling Him how to change my husband. I had to stop trying to do God's job.

The Spirit used David's words like a balm for mending my heart: "Let the morning bring me word of your unfailing love, for I have put my trust in you. Show me the way I should go, for to you I entrust my life" (Psalm 143:8). David's prayer pricked the depths of my soul. I inhaled: "Teach me to do your will, for you are my God; may your good Spirit lead me on level ground" (v. 10). I exhaled: Holy Spirit, I am Yours. I'm ready. I am willing. Do what You will.

I used to cringe at the thought of spiritual transformation because change is often uncomfortable and even painful, especially when the change means giving up my way. Surrendering to the Holy Spirit demanded that I stop trying to control everything. Placing Christ as Lord over every aspect of my life would cause discomfort, lead to loss, and force me to give up my battle stance. Surrendering to the Spirit meant my world would no longer revolve around my wants or expectations, my opinions or preferences. But love requires sacrifice, submission, and obedience.

When our desires change from getting our way to pleasing God by living His way, we won't need to understand God's reasons. We won't need to win every earthly battle. We can view the war with an eternal perspective, the war Jesus already won when He defeated our true enemy—the devil.

The Holy Spirit will not fight one of God's image-bearers on our behalf. He will lead us, but He won't make us follow Him. He will transform us when we submit to His authority, but He won't bend us to His will. He will protect us and provide for us, but He won't make us receive His refuge. He will give us all we need to walk with Him by faith and in victory, but He won't force us to ask for help or receive and rely on His power. God waits for us to trust Him. He gives us enough grace to request all we need to surrender and follow Him one sacred stride at a time, no matter where His path for us leads.

Inhale

> Teach me to do your will,
>   for you are my God;
> may your good Spirit
>   lead me on level ground.
> (Psalm 143:10)

Exhale

Wonderful Counselor, thanks for reminding us that we cannot change ourselves or anyone else. Help us raise our hands in complete surrender, trusting You will always do all things for the good of *all* who love You. Please keep us from succumbing to our human frailty and striving to feel stronger, fearless, and in control. Instead, show us all we need to release as we accept that You are truly all we need. May Your will be done and Your power magnified in and through our weaknesses as You work in and through our relationships with You and others. In Jesus's name, amen.

SACRED STRIDE

Admit your desperate and continual need for the Holy Spirit to help you honor God in and through your relationships. Then ask Him to help you submit to Him so you can obey Him and trust Him to work as He sees fit, as you pray for the people you love by name.

3

Accepting New Life

STEP INTO GOD'S WORD
2 Corinthians 5:11–6:2

STAND ON GOD'S TRUTH
*The Holy Spirit uses our old life to equip us
for the new life He's planned for us.*

When an unwed young woman discovered she was pregnant, a family member suggested that it would be best if she had an abortion. Distressed, she shared the news with the baby's father. He intervened and, to her surprise, proposed. The young couple tried to make their marriage work. They loved their daughter, Shadia, and the son they had two years later. But when Shadia was only twelve years old, they divorced.

Shadia doesn't remember when she started questioning her self-worth. However, she will never forget the fear that overcame her when she discovered she was pregnant at the age of fifteen. The nurse told her that the life she carried in her womb was not a child. Her mother said it would be best if she got an abortion. Sadly, no one intervened for the life of Shadia's baby.

Soon after her mother and stepfather took her to an abortion clinic, Shadia spiraled into a life of trying to numb her emotional pain through drinking, promiscuity, and drug abuse. Grief and shame haunted her. As she struggled with suicidal thoughts, her lifestyle led her into dangerous spaces. At only seventeen years of age, Shadia was date-raped.

Lost and desperate for comfort, she moved in with an abusive man before her eighteenth birthday. She married him seven years later and soon learned that she could not have children. Shadia believed her heartbreaking infertility was a direct result of the abortion she had as a teenager.

When Shadia was thirty, her husband suggested they accept a friend's invitation to a Bible study. She had always thought the concept of a loving God felt like a fairy tale—too good to be true. She planned on just going along for the ride. But six months later, her husband stopped drinking. When she witnessed her husband's transformation, God had Shadia's full attention.

Shadia had lots of questions. She accepted that she was a sinner who needed saving, so she dove into the Bible to learn more about God. After placing her faith in Christ, she began telling everyone about this real God who was changing their lives. Not long afterward, though, her husband returned to his old ways and filed for divorce. Shadia struggled with confusion and grief, but continued learning about God and talking about Him with anyone who would listen.

Sadly, it didn't take long before Shadia also sank back into her life of sin. She didn't understand why she went back to a lifestyle she didn't want. She cried out to God and eventually realized that while she had embraced Jesus as Savior, she hadn't truly surrendered to Jesus as Lord. She confessed, asked God to forgive her and to be Lord of her life. In turn, she experienced His grace and forgiveness.

As she continued to study the Bible, Shadia was drawn to the stories of the overlooked, undervalued, and often unseen people in Scripture. She wanted to learn more about how God had worked in and through their lives. As she studied the story of Tamar in Genesis 38, the Holy Spirit began a mighty work of healing in Shadia. God comforted her as she reflected on how He redeemed Tamar, even including her in the genealogy of Jesus despite her sinful choices. Shadia saw Tamar's story as a demonstration of God's loving mercy, leading to a transformed life used for His glory.

Believing God would redeem and use her too, Shadia committed to sharing her story. She began introducing others to the messy stories of the Bible's unsung heroes, the men and women who experienced deep hurt and trauma. She went back to school, received a master's degree in biblical and theological studies, and began using writing and speaking to serve God. She even began speaking against abortion with love and compassion. However, Shadia continued struggling with the way she viewed herself.

The Holy Spirit began revealing that her insecurities were based on the Enemy's lies about her past, her identity, and her worth. He helped her combat those lies with Scripture. On one side of a small notecard, Shadia would write a lie she believed; then on the other side, she wrote a Bible verse refuting that lie. The more the Spirit confirmed Shadia's identity as God's renewed and redeemed daughter, the less she felt the need to hide her scars.

With every detail of Shadia's past known, forgiven, and redeemed by Jesus's love, the Holy Spirit affirmed that her old life did not define her worth or reflect her future. The more she grew to know the Father's heart intimately and experience Jesus's love personally, the more she longed to know Him and make Him known.

However, she had learned from her past experiences. She knew she could not move forward depending on her own abilities or accomplishments. Shadia relied on the Holy Spirit for everything because she had to, not just because she wanted to or because Scripture said she should. As God provided for all her needs, He empowered Shadia to walk in victory, live her new life in Christ and for Christ, and passionately share His Word.

The apostle Paul says that Christ's love "compels" us to live for Him because of His death and resurrection (2 Corinthians 5:14–15). Paul is saying the love of Christ is so overwhelming that we're compelled, meaning "forced" or "driven," to be totally committed in every aspect of our lives to Christ and Christ alone. We are designed with a purpose and propelled to live as if Christ is the one and only Lord in our lives. That is impossible to do without the power of the Holy Spirit.

Believers in Jesus are reconciled *through* Christ, who no longer holds our sins against us, so we can live our new lives *for* Christ as His representatives (vv. 18–20). To die to ourselves means to leave our sinfulness and our soul scars in the mighty and merciful healing hands of our Savior, Jesus Christ. When He rose from that tomb, Jesus defeated death. Period. As the Holy Spirit raises us up in victory with Christ, the dead moments of our past become the proof of His life-changing love. Every time we inhale His truth and exhale prayers and praises, we are proclaiming our new lives in Him. Testifying is also a way of welcoming others to encounter God, receive Christ as their Savior and Lord, and invite the Holy Spirit to change their lives, just as He has changed and is changing our lives.

Over time, as we seek to know God better, relying on Him as we study His Word and submit to Him, we will be transformed. The Holy Spirit aligns our hearts and minds with

Jesus, whose heart and mind are revealed through His whole story—the Bible. In an overflow of loving mercy and gentleness, the Spirit helps us to increasingly reflect Christ's character and become living testimonies.

God's unerring and unchanging truth—Scripture—destroys the Enemy's lies that once bound us. The labels that limited us are gone. The shame and guilt that weighed us down are in the past. Having stepped out of our old life the moment we accepted Christ and received the Holy Spirit, we can walk with confidence in the new life God planned for each of us while we were still in our mother's womb. With our eyes fixed on Jesus and our hearts overflowing with praises, we can receive and share His love and truth in every circumstance, wherever, whenever, and however He leads.

Hallelujah!

Inhale

If anyone is in Christ, the new creation has come: The old has gone, the new is here! (2 Corinthians 5:17)

Exhale

Life-transforming Spirit, thanks for knowing us intimately and never dwelling on our past sins. Please heal the wounds caused by the sins of others and also those festering sores we've caused by giving in to our fleshly desires and justifying, minimizing, or glorifying our own sins. Reveal and eradicate the sins that still hinder us from living the abundant life You promise—a life devoted to honoring You, not pleasing ourselves. Please provide all we need to share our testimony without shame, giving You all the glory as we live for You and share Your Word with confidence and expectant faith. In Jesus's name, amen.

SACRED STRIDE

Confess the ways you are still living in the flesh or in bondage to the limitations of your past. Then ask the Holy Spirit to empower you to embrace the freedom of your new life through Christ as your Lord.

4

Receiving and Relying on the Spirit

STEP INTO GOD'S WORD
John 20:19–23

STAND ON GOD'S TRUTH
*The Holy Spirit waits for us to receive Him
so He can be our power source.*

Raised in a church pew of a Black church during the Jim Crow era, Patricia confessed to being angry about racial injustice as a young adult. She struggled with racial hate, especially toward White people. But she felt the Holy Spirit tugging her heart to forgive. Though forgiveness seemed impossible, Patricia submitted to the Holy Spirit and obeyed. She never expected that the lessons God used to help her with racial healing and forgiveness would be pivotal in her own family dynamics when she became a mother.

After her Christian daughter converted to Islam, Patricia felt like a failure as a Christian parent. While the Enemy tried to condemn her of not doing enough, God affirmed that *He* was doing enough. She couldn't change what she did or didn't do in the past, but she could trust God with her life and the lives of her loved ones. As the Holy Spirit filled her with His love, He enabled Patricia to be present and show love even though she did not agree with her daughter's choices. Committed to spending time with her daughter, she invited her into conversations without being combative. More importantly, she trusted God to work out their tension as an interfaith family.

At first Patricia still wanted to tell her daughter what to do. She struggled with yielding to the Holy Spirit but was willing. One choice at a time, He enabled her to rely on Him to change her heart and the way she communicated with her daughter. As love began to relieve the tensions in her family, Patricia realized that every person was at a different place on their spiritual journey. This awareness changed her relationship with God, her daughter, and every other person going forward.

Through her continual Bible reading and prayer, the Spirit changed the way Patricia saw, heard, and loved her daughter. Patricia knew that Jesus loved her and wanted her to love others because of His love for her. She wanted to love her daughter for the same reason, not because of her daughter's compliance to her wishes. She also knew that God loved her daughter, so she asked Him to help her stop arguing and condemning the child He had entrusted to her.

The Holy Spirit transformed her thinking. He helped Patricia listen to and love her daughter while relying on Him to do what only He could do. When Patricia stopped believing it was her responsibility to fix people, she grew closer to God and others. She began to understand that God was not passive. He was not depending on her or anyone else to do His job.

Whenever Patricia became overcome by worry, stumped by unforgiveness, or upset about the people and things she could not change, she pulled out a piece of paper and drew a vertical line down the middle of the page. On the side labeled "Thank You, God," she listed things that she was grateful for in that moment. On the other side labeled "Give to God," she wrote the things she needed to surrender to Him. Then she prayed. Trusting that everything was in God's hands, she could live and sleep in the peace of His constant presence.

Patricia finally realized that after making her beliefs known to her daughter there was no need to continue repeating herself or arguing on God's behalf. The Holy Spirit was the only one who could bring anyone to Christ. So she chose to love her family while praying for them. Though her daughter still practices Islam, Patricia enjoys spending time with her and building relationships with her grandchildren. She even partnered with her daughter to write a book about their experiences.

The fragrant fruit of her relationship with her daughter wasn't a result of Patricia's choices or willingness to do better. The fruit of the Spirit, which became evident in her relationships, was cultivated by the Spirit Himself while He was working in and through her life. As Patricia studied God's Word and prayed, the Holy Spirit enabled her to submit to His authority, live for Jesus, and love like Jesus. She understood and believed that God could use her to draw others closer to Christ, but He wasn't reliant on her to do so. She embraced God's perfect plan and pace for her growth and the growth of those she loves. And the rich relationships with her daughter and her grandchildren have continued to flourish as an overflow of the fruit of the Spirit flourishing in Patricia's life.

The apostle John tells believers how to access the infinite power of God the Spirit and how to do our job as lovers of God and people. After the Roman soldiers crucified Jesus and buried him in a tomb, Jesus rose, stood among His disciples, and said, "Peace be with you!" (John 20:19). Jesus shared His blessing of tranquility and showed the disciples His scarred hands and side, an action that represented more than providing proof of life. His gesture proved His divine identity. "The disciples were overjoyed when they saw the Lord" (v. 20). Their enthusiastic response to seeing Jesus came after thinking their hopes had been dashed on the cross and in the tomb. What Jesus did next was an extravagant act of love that set the precedent for how He expected His disciples to live out their faith on this side of eternity.

"Again Jesus said, 'Peace be with you! As the Father has sent me, I am sending you.' And with that he breathed on them and said, 'Receive the Holy Spirit'" (v. 22). The Greek word for "receive" in this verse, *lambanō*, means "to take," "take possession of," or "seize," which are not passive actions.* The word *lambanō* can also be used in reference to being married, as in receiving a bride or groom, which signifies a beautiful depth of intimacy. Knowing the disciples would not be able to fulfill their purpose in their own strength, Jesus—God in the flesh—breathed on them, and the Spirit became all they needed to fulfill their purpose. The breath of God, referred to in Genesis 2:7, is the actual breath of *life*. Through Jesus's extraordinary interaction with the disciples, the Advocate who would be with and in them always would become their intimate, immediately accessible power source . . . and so much more.

Jesus didn't tell the disciples to just believe in the Holy Spirit. He was telling the disciples that they needed to take hold of the Holy Spirit and experience a relationship. By indwelling us, the Spirit opens Himself to be personally acknowledged and understood, to be welcomed and met with,

* John R. Kohlenberger, *The NIV Exhaustive Bible Concordance*, 3rd ed. (Grand Rapids, MI: Zondervan, 2015), s.v. "G3284 lambanō."

to be accepted and loved, and to be trusted. The disciples needed to deliberately activate the relationship Jesus offered them with the Spirit. They were invited to greet the Advocate with each breath they took. We also are invited to greet Him with every breath we take.

After blessing the disciples with the Holy Spirit, Jesus empowered them to forgive (v. 23). If the disciples believed in God the Son and received God the Spirit, they would be able to forgive as they had been forgiven. However, Jesus knew that to live and love as He lived and loved, His disciples would require supernatural, unlimited, and always accessible assistance.

When we place our trust in Jesus as our Savior *and* submit to Him as our Lord, we can call on His Spirit with confidence. We can reach out and welcome Him to transform our hearts so that we can love when we want to hate. We can invite Him to change our minds and tame our tongues so we can be peacemakers who listen and pray when we want to argue. The Spirit will make Jesus known through us, and He will make us known as Jesus's own to those around us. We can walk by faith, filling every sacred space with compassion and prayers that become love transactions. As we recognize that our power source is our very breath of life, we can call on Him with every breath we take.

Holy Spirit, I am ready and willing. Come have Your way in me!

Inhale

> Again Jesus said, "Peace be with you! As the Father has sent me, I am sending you." And with that he breathed on them and said, "Receive the Holy Spirit." (John 20:21–22)

Exhale

Mighty Advocate, thanks for rooting our faith in Your limitless abilities and constant availability. Change our hearts so we can love others as abundantly and unconditionally as You love us. Give us words to share the truth of Scripture with gentleness and respect as we pray for others. Enable us to listen well, respect our differences, forgive, and live as peacemakers. And please help us trust that You will transform us and others in Your way and in Your timing, as You use us to draw others to You by the way we love. In Jesus's name, amen.

SACRED STRIDE

Ask the Holy Spirit to reveal every relationship with the people you have previously judged, condemned, attempted to fix, and refused to forgive. Then ask the Holy Spirit to provide all you need so that you can forgive, seek forgiveness, and love others as genuinely and generously as He loves you.

5

Always and Forever

STEP INTO GOD'S WORD
Romans 8:18–39

STAND ON GOD'S TRUTH
The Holy Spirit maintains an open line of communication.

My six-year-old son, Xavier, and I arrived at the nursing home for our weekly visit. He slid out of the back seat with his backpack and a large piece of cardstock. I grabbed my Bible and the paper bag filled with my mother-in-law's favorite fast-food lunch.

Reaching for Xavier's hand, I reminded him that Grandma probably wouldn't remember who we were. He adjusted one of the shoulder straps of his backpack and said, "I know. She has Old-Timer's disease."

I smiled and said, "Alzheimer's."

Xavier scrunched his brows and assured me that I was repeating exactly what he said. Holding up the picture he'd painted for his grandmother earlier that week, he said, "This will help her remember."

I exhaled a silent prayer. Why can't life be that simple, Lord?

When we arrived at the door, Xavier showed the nurse his love offering.

She clasped her hands and told him the gift would look perfect on his grandma's wall. Handing me a pen to sign the visitor's log, she told us that Grandma Dixon had a rough morning with lots of tears but was feeling better.

Xavier sighed heavily and said, "My pictures make her happy, like she used to be."

I tasted the grief at the heart of his innocent comment. He used to enjoy visiting his grandmother in her home. As a retired teacher, she always had plenty of snacks and art supplies. He talked. She listened. They laughed. Then they picked fruit from the trees growing in her back yard. Xavier always asked for five more minutes when I announced we had to leave. Grandma Dixon always pretended she couldn't let him go when they hugged and said goodbye. We visited regularly until the day she walked out of her house, drove off in her car, and couldn't find her way home. That could-have-been-so-much-worse event led to the diagnosis that changed our lives and her home address.

We stopped by the doorway before entering the eating area. The nurse approached a frail woman staring at the wall with a slight frown on her face and announced visitors. My mother-in-law blinked several times and said she had to get ready for school.

The nurse assured her that she had plenty of time and waved us over to the table.

When Xavier handed Grandma Dixon the picture he'd drawn, she welcomed him into a big hug and said, "You're such a kind boy. You get an A-plus in my class."

Dropping his bag on the floor, he sat in the chair next to his grandmother and told her that he always got good grades.

Grandma Dixon patted my hand when I set our lunch on the table and thanked me for sharing. Then she asked if Xavier was my son.

I nodded, smiling as I blinked away tears and prayed silently.

Xavier told his grandmother about his week as she nibbled her food. He talked. She listened. They laughed.

When I finished eating, I pulled out my Bible and asked if Xavier remembered where we had left off.

He took his Bible out of his backpack and reminded me it was his turn to read.

My mother-in-law snagged a tiny lint ball off her sweater. Her gaze zoomed in on the piece of fabric she rolled in between her thumb and index finger.

Xavier cleared his throat and began reading the God-breathed words of Scripture, using the dramatic flair that he'd inherited from me. "Psalm one hundred. 'Shout for joy to the LORD, all the earth. Worship the LORD with gladness; come before him with joyful songs.'"

Grandma Dixon looked into Xavier's eyes, raised one hand, and said, "Hallelujah!"

My son opened his mouth, as if to speak, then pressed his lips together. He rose slowly from his chair, gently wrapped his arms around his grandmother's neck, and laid his head on her shoulder.

She rocked slightly. Patting her grandson's back, she hummed a familiar hymn.

I whispered, "Hallelujah."

As my mother-in-law's health declined, the Holy Spirit continued reminding me of that moment. I still believe that the biblical truth she knew after decades of reading, teaching, singing, and believing His Word was not stolen by the disease when she couldn't recite Scripture anymore. Those sparks of recognition, though sometimes small, occurred when we sang or listened to worship music or read the Bible to her. The presence of God's Word tucked deep into her heart, which beat in sync with the heart of God the Father, proved the faithfulness of God the Spirit in affirming that her hope remained secure in God the Son. Even when she couldn't tell us that she remembered Him, God remembered her.

Grandma Dixon could not identify us as family members that day or for the days that followed. However, her responses to the reading or singing of God's living and active Word assured me that she could still recognize God's voice by the Spirit who dwelled in her.

The apostle Paul wrote, "I consider that our present sufferings are not worth comparing with the glory that will be revealed in us" (Romans 8:18). Paul never denied, minimized, or justified the wretched, sin-ridden state of the world or the difficult circumstances from which he preached. Yet he never lost hope in the future glory promised through a life-changing relationship with Christ. He proclaimed that "the creation itself will be liberated from its bondage to decay and brought into the freedom and glory of the children of God" (v. 21). His declaration of faith reaches into the depths of hopelessness. He revealed an inexplicable peace secured in the proven faithfulness of our ever-present Helper—God the Holy Spirit. The apostle declared believers in Jesus are citizens of heaven longing for the "redemption of our bodies" (vv. 22–23).

While we're faith-walking as foreigners on this earth, there will be moments when we won't know what to pray or how to pray. There will be seasons when we have no strength to utter the name of Jesus out loud. There may even be times when we or someone we care for will lose the desire or the ability to communicate with people and with God. But there will never be a moment when God severs the line of communication with His children, those who have placed their trust in Jesus as Savior and Lord.

The apostle Paul declared with unshakable conviction that the Holy Spirit "helps us in our weakness" and "intercedes for us through wordless groans" (v. 26). Yes! Because Jesus, God the Son, "lives forever, he has a permanent priesthood. Therefore he is able to save completely those who come to God through him, because he always lives to intercede for them. Such a high priest truly meets our need—one who is holy, blameless, pure, set apart from sinners, exalted above the heavens" (Hebrews 7:24–26).

On this side of eternity, when our lamenting has been silenced to incomprehensible groans, we can count on the Holy Spirit to maintain an open line of communication with us. He stands in the gap for us. As God the Father searches our hearts, He simultaneously knows our hearts completely through the Spirit. He "knows the mind of the Spirit, because the Spirit intercedes for God's people in accordance with the will of God" (Romans 8:27).

The Holy Spirit never breaks contact with us. He never loses sight of us. He never stops hearing us. He never stops knowing us. He never stops arbitrating for us. Even when we're unable to acknowledge, accept, or articulate our innermost feelings and needs, we can trust the Holy Spirit. He will maintain an open line of clear and consistent communication with us and for us forever.

In all circumstances in the lives of all believers around the world, we can count on God to remain true to His promises. "We know that in all things God works for the good of those who love him, who have been called according to his purpose" (v. 28). To God be the glory, the honor, and the praise!

Inhale

In the same way, the Spirit helps us in our weakness. We do not know what we ought to pray for, but the Spirit himself intercedes for us through wordless groans. (Romans 8:26)

Exhale

Listening and interceding Spirit, thanks for affirming that our weaknesses and limitations on this side of eternity only provide opportunities for You to do everything You promise. Engrain the assurance of Your reliability deep into our hearts and minds. Thanks for never breaking contact with us, never letting us go, and never leaving us to fend for ourselves during battles we were never meant to fight. Be our peace in the silence. Give us strength to be still and trust that You know us and our needs, even when we can't express or understand them on our own. In Jesus's name, amen.

SACRED STRIDE

Practice breathing prayers using Bible verses that affirm the Holy Spirit's constant presence. Slow your breathing as you read silently. Then inhale as you receive the truth and exhale prayers and praises. End by thanking and praising God.

Accurate Reflection

STEP INTO GOD'S WORD
Judges 6:1–24

STAND ON GOD'S TRUTH
*The Holy Spirit provides an accurate reflection
of who we are because of Christ.*

As a senior in high school, Faith strived to become the best discus thrower as she trained and dreamed of competing in the Olympics. She also invested in nurturing her personal relationship with God. She first read through the whole Bible in the eighth grade and began setting an alarm to wake up at 4:30 a.m. so she could study the Bible before starting her day. Eager to know God's Word, Faith wrote Bible verses on sticky notes and placed them all over the house. As she developed her spiritual muscles, she looked and felt physically healthy and strong too—until one morning during her senior year in high school. Without warning or previous symptoms, Faith woke up and couldn't get out of bed. Though she hadn't injured herself, she knew something was wrong.

Faith's normally positive attitude about life became negative as her parents prayed and doctors failed to provide answers or relief. After trying several procedures over the next few months, her condition worsened. Doctors told Faith that she could not participate in track and field anymore. They recommended that she seriously consider a plan B. Faith grieved the loss of her health and her dream of competing in the Olympics. She loved God and knew He was with her. So she couldn't understand why He was taking everything away from her. Distancing herself from family, friends, and God for over a year, Faith sunk deeper into despair. Eventually she stopped reading the Bible and praying.

Over a year and a half later, doctors discovered that Faith had fractured her spine while throwing the discus. After her third stem-cell procedure, Faith's body began healing, but her battle with depression worsened. While her parents continued supporting her physical healing, they took her to a Christian therapist. Also, without pressuring Faith in a way she would have resented, they held her hands to pray with her, left a Bible available and open on the kitchen table, and gently reminded Faith to turn to God. As time passed, even while doctors insisted Faith stop participating in track and field, she began to feel God's presence again. She graduated high school and went on to college, trusting that her walk with God would take her further than track and field or any plan B.

While living away from home during her first year of college, Faith leaned on God. She read her Bible, prayed, and sang praise and worship songs. As she began feeling better physically and emotionally, she eased into training with doctor supervision. After she started throwing again, her outlook improved. Then, without warning, she began struggling with anxiety and depression again.

Faith committed to the daily spiritual habits she had in place before her health crisis began. She set her alarm clock and, even when she didn't feel like it, got up to read the Bible and pray. As weariness and worry overcame her, she couldn't understand why all her efforts weren't working. She cried out to God.

And God showed up.

After transferring to another school for her second year of college, with the support of her family, doctors, coaches, and friends, Faith returned to training and competing. By God's grace, Faith made it to the US Championships in 2023 and competed in the Olympic Trials in 2024. Though she didn't qualify, Faith knew she could trust God and looked forward to training for the 2028 Olympics.

At age twenty-two, Faith understood that her identity shouldn't be tied to her aspirations, accomplishments, or ability to participate in any activity. Though she's still figuring out how to keep God first, she's not trying to do anything in her own strength anymore. Faith seeks God for wisdom. She relies on Him and accepts the loving support of others as she moves forward in hope. She's making her needs a priority by getting up early and spending time with God as she starts her day. She sets her alarm clock, not to remind herself to make time for God but so she can have time to enjoy connecting with Him as she prayerfully reads the Scriptures. With her identity secure in Christ, Faith no longer tries to achieve self-care by depending on *self*-help.

God's people have a history of struggling to keep God first and of doing things in their own strength. Even those we might consider the most faithful of His servant-leaders grapple with doubt and bad cases of self-sufficiency. One such leader, Gideon, lived in the chaos caused by the rebellion of God's people. Scripture says the "Israelites did evil in the eyes of the LORD, and for seven years he gave them into the hands of the

Midianites" (Judges 6:1). When the Israelites cried out to God, he sent a prophet to remind them of how they betrayed Him through their blatant displays of idolatry (vv. 7–10).

Gideon had grown up in a culture steeped in sin, a culture bound under this prolonged oppression due to an entire community's willful disobedience to God. Gideon's home was no different—his father owned idols (v. 25). But even if his whole family had managed to avoid idolatry, the culture would have impacted him physically, mentally, emotionally, and even spiritually in some way or another. But God entered into this young man's life—and everything changed.

> When the angel of the LORD appeared to Gideon, he said, "The LORD is with you, mighty warrior."
>
> "Pardon me, my lord," Gideon replied, "but if the LORD is with us, why has all this happened to us? Where are all his wonders that our ancestors told us about when they said, 'Did not the LORD bring us up out of Egypt?' But now the LORD has abandoned us and given us into the hand of Midian" (v. 12–13).

Skipping right over the declaration of his identity as a "mighty warrior," Gideon dove into the promise. If God is with us, where's the proof? Why have we been suffering? Where are His wonders we've heard about from generation to generation?

God didn't dignify Gideon's sarcasm with a response. Instead, "the LORD turned to him and said, 'Go in the strength you have and save Israel out of Midian's hand. Am I not sending you?'" (v. 14). The strength Gideon possessed would be sufficient because God Himself was doing the sending and the strengthening.

Still, this "mighty warrior" focused on his dire circumstances,

50

low status, and lack of resources (v. 15). God's reply was simple and direct: "I will be with you" (v. 16). And to Gideon's doubt, God responded with loving patience (v. 17).

Later, Gideon would serve as a judge, entrusted to lead God's people against their enemies. He would serve as a prophet, believed to speak the very words from God's mouth as a messenger. And his name would be recorded in the book of Hebrews' hall of faith (11:32–34).

Whenever God's people suffer from an identity crisis, we drift from our true source of life, distort communication with our source of wisdom, and disconnect with our source of power—God in us. Consumed with the suffering that seems endless in that moment, we forget that God secures our hope in His promise to remain with us, in us, and in control always and forever. We try harder because we doubt God will show up. We hold on tighter because we're afraid God won't hold on to us if we let go. We worry because we're not sure God is listening to our prayers. We bow our heads in shame because we're afraid His grace is only sufficient for our neighbors, who don't seem to have as many skeletons living in their closets as we do.

But God has proven His faithfulness and goodness. He offers us sanity-saving peace if only we'll confess and turn away from our sins and accept the gift of Christ's forgiveness. God's grace is sufficient, which means adequate, necessary, and enough. If we acknowledge our desperate and ongoing need for Him, we can do a trust-fall of faith into His unyielding embrace.

When we focus daily on God instead of ourselves, the Holy Spirit gives us an accurate reflection of who we are in Him. We can always be battle ready, taking each sacred stride as mighty faith warriors guaranteed to have God the Spirit with us.

Inhale

> When the angel of the LORD appeared to Gideon,
> he said, "The LORD is with you, mighty warrior."
> (Judges 6:12)

Exhale

Holy Spirit, please make us brave and mighty warriors who recognize Your voice distinctly and stand firmly on the trustworthy words You preserved in the whole Bible. Give us an accurate reflection of who we are because of who You are and all You've done for us. Thanks for using every weak moment in the wilderness to affirm that self-help leads to self-destruction. Increase our desire and diligence in connecting with You while trusting Your unyielding connection with us. Help us trust that true self-care begins and ends by fueling ourselves with Your truth and depending on Your power. In Jesus's name, amen.

SACRED STRIDE

Ask the Holy Spirit to help you memorize Scripture that affirms the truth about your identity in Christ, your purpose as a Christ follower, and your Spirit-empowered mighty warrior status.

7

Ever-Present Everywhere

STEP INTO GOD'S WORD
Acts 17:16–31

STAND ON GOD'S TRUTH
*The Holy Spirit goes wherever we go
and wherever we can't reach.*

The front-page story with a full-color picture popped up on my computer screen. Police officers had their guns aimed at a young Black man with his arms raised. Even with a bandanna covering the lower half of his face, I recognized my almost nineteen-year-old relative.

Dazed, I called my husband then contacted the local police station. I quickly discovered what little rights I had to get information about an eighteen-year-old adult. When my husband refused to visit the jail, I asked a few close friends to pray for us, picked up my Bible, and went into our bedroom to pray.

I asked God to change my husband's heart toward one so

dear to us. I could understand how my relative's decision-making might not have been as easy as wanting to do the right things. The pain of life on this side of eternity often blinds us from receiving God's perfect love or anyone else's flawed attempts to love us. As angry as I was, my scarred soul understood his plight.

I opened my Bible, stretched across my bed, and prayed as I flipped through the pages. I knew exactly where the Holy Spirit was leading me. As I read the red words splattered across the page, my heart grew heavier:

> Then the King will say to those on his right, "Come, you who are blessed by my Father; take your inheritance, the kingdom prepared for you since the creation of the world. For I was hungry and you gave me something to eat, I was thirsty and you gave me something to drink, I was a stranger and you invited me in, I needed clothes and you clothed me, I was sick and you looked after me, I was in prison and you came to visit me." (Matthew 25:34–36)

You? I was quite familiar with the text. I knew what came next.

> Then the righteous will answer him, "Lord, when did we see you hungry and feed you, or thirsty and give you something to drink? When did we see you a stranger and invite you in, or needing clothes and clothe you? When did we see you sick or in prison and go to visit you?" (vv. 37–39)

The Holy Spirit nudged me. *You. Go.*
I frowned and continued reading.

The King will reply, "Truly I tell you, whatever you did for one of the least of these brothers and sisters of mine, you did *for me*." (v. 40, emphasis mine)

My relative was one of "the least of these," meaning a person who had placed his trust in Christ. I wanted to make excuses and justify my inability to forgive his past sins. Instead, the Holy Spirit pricked my heart with compassion. He reminded me that sin is sin, and my sin of choice was no less sinful. Then He took me straight to the words of Jesus: "If you love me, keep my commands. And I will ask the Father, and he will give you another advocate to help you and be with you forever—the Spirit of truth. The world cannot accept him, because it neither sees him nor knows him. But you know him, for he lives with you and will be in you" (John 14:15–17).

I picked up my Bible, walked into the living room, and read the verses to my husband. I told him that I would be obeying God and invited him to join me.

The next day I drove across town alone.

I prayed for the people around me until a security guard led a small group of us into a room with chairs and counter cubicles with phones. I watched through smudged glass as a guard led the six-foot-five young man to meet with me. He picked up the receiver, then placed his large palm on the thick glass, fingers splayed.

I wept when I heard his voice through the plastic phone. "I'm sorry," he said. "Please don't cry." As I pulled my hand away from the cold glass, I didn't see a criminal in prison garb. I saw a young man I loved and couldn't hug. "I'm crying because I can't help you while you're in there," I said. But I knew who could help him.

God would not abandon my loved on in his time of need.

So I made sure he would be slinging Scripture while scuffling with the Enemy during hand-to-hand combat in the dark corners of that jail cell. I bought him the *Celebrate Recovery Bible* on my way home. The next day, I arranged for the chaplain to place that brand-new sword of truth into his young hands.

The Holy Spirit continued working on our hearts as I prayed. My husband joined me on my next visit to the county jail. We encouraged our beloved relative to follow the same daily Bible reading schedule we were using. We promised to support him and provide a place to stay after he was released. One condition: He had to tell the truth throughout the entire process. He did.

I believed our loved one received Christ during a youth camp at the age of fifteen. However, even if he hadn't, I knew God would hear every prayer I uttered on his behalf. God would speak to him through the Scriptures he'd heard spoken in church, at our home, and through the Bible the chaplain had delivered for us. Nothing—not concrete walls secured by guards, not even the walls he had built around his broken heart—could separate him from the God who loved him un-conditionally before he was even born. God didn't need me to fix this situation. God didn't need me to protect this teen. God didn't need me to do anything. All I needed to do was love this young man, pray for him, and wait for the Holy Spirit to do a mighty work in him, in my husband, and in me. God's still working on us and on our relationships.

When the apostle Paul addressed the people of Athens in Acts 17, he said, "The God who made the world and everything in it is the Lord of heaven and earth and does not live in temples built by human hands. And he is not served by human hands, as if he needed anything. Rather, he himself gives everyone life and breath and everything else. From one man he made all the nations, that they should inhabit the whole earth; and he marked out their appointed times in history and the boundaries of their lands. God did this so that they would seek him and perhaps reach out for him and find him, though he is not far from any one of us. 'For in him we live and move and have our being'" (Acts 17:24–28).

By God's incredible grace, our loved one spent his twenty-first birthday celebrating with our family and our church family. That night I cried after he went to bed, sober and safe in our home. I praised Jesus for giving all of us our *next* chance. Years have passed. That young man is now thriving as a gainfully employed husband and father who loves his family.

Though it's often tempting to force a quick fix when times are challenging, the Holy Spirit uses the Scriptures to comfort and guide us. Jesus Himself leads us into the sacred space of forgiveness. He infuses us with hope when we have no power to help our loved ones or ourselves. Even those who are not believers are never out of our faithful Father's reach when we shield them with prayers. So, no matter where we are in life or what is happening, we can trust that no one is too far for God to see, hear, touch, and love.

Inhale

> From one man he made all the nations, that they should inhabit the whole earth; and he marked out their appointed times in history and the boundaries of their lands. God did this so that they would seek him and perhaps reach out for him and find him, though he is not far from any one of us. (Acts 17:26–27)

Exhale

Ever-present Spirit of God, thanks for affirming Your unchanging promises, Your unconditional love, and Your unyielding presence throughout Scripture and in every intimate space in our lives. Thanks for giving us every *next* chance as You work in us and in our relationships. Help us remember that You remain with us wherever we go and wherever we cannot reach. In Jesus's name, amen.

SACRED STRIDE

Ask the Holy Spirit to reveal Himself to you and to those you love who feel out of reach as He does a miracle of mercy, providing *next* chances and reconciliation in and through your relationships.

8

Cease and Submit

STEP INTO GOD'S WORD
Romans 7:18–8:17

STAND ON GOD'S TRUTH
The Holy Spirit won't let us down no matter
where He has us in this present moment.

A broken engagement in her early twenties became a catalyst that increased Amy's desire to grow closer to God. As she grieved the loss of her relationship, she experienced an increasing desire to read the Bible. Over the next five years, she enjoyed communing with God and developed a deeper intimacy with Him. She also eventually began praying for a new romantic relationship. God answered that prayer only six days before her thirtieth birthday, when she married an English man. He swept her off her feet and whisked her over four thousand miles away. The couple planned to spend five to seven years in the United Kingdom, then return to America. Amy got what she wanted, but she had to leave everything and everyone behind.

While enjoying her new marriage and adjusting to the

new culture, Amy supported her husband in his role of serving the church. Soon, however, a sense of loss and loneliness overwhelmed her. For an entire month she prayed that God would give her a friend. Experience had taught her that some people in her new community might be uncomfortable with her outgoing personality. But desperation for connection made her willing to risk rejection. She intentionally used her perceived friendly "American-ness" to break down barriers. And in His perfect timing, God sent her three friends who were members of her church.

Amy began investing in building relationships with the women God had sent her. Giving of herself took time, but eventually she saw the beginning foundations of genuine friendships. As a minister's wife, however, the pressures of spoken and unspoken expectations weighed on her. She still wondered if she was too loud. She worried that she always seemed to do the wrong thing. As their family grew, she continued feeling out of place. She struggled to overcome her fear of embarrassing her husband and their two children. Amy longed to return to the States, to her home, so she cried out to God repeatedly.

Some years later, Amy received an opportunity to spend some time at a Christian retreat center. Her husband prayed over her before she left, asking God to give her clarity about living in the United States or in the UK. Amy wrestled with her husband's words. They had a plan, a deal, an agreement about how long they would stay in Britain. Her excitement about the retreat deflated before she walked out the door. She decided to begin what she called her "campaign" to convince God and her husband to take her home.

At the retreat center, Amy read her Bible and wrote in her prayer journal. She campaigned for their return to America while overlooking a wonderful view of a lake. One day she felt the Holy Spirit clearly telling her to give up her campaign. Amy slammed her journal shut. She wanted to live in America. She didn't want to ignore God's voice, but she couldn't stop wrestling with Him either. She believed God loved her. She knew He was good. He had always come through for her. Desperate to please Him, Amy asked God to help her trust His character and listen to His guidance.

After the retreat, the Holy Spirit enabled Amy to surrender her campaign. She released everything to God. And He began extending her friendships through a global community. In 2015 she began writing for Our Daily Bread Ministries and also released her first book. Bursting with gratitude and joy, Amy praised God and poured herself into her relationship with Him and the people He sent into her life.

One day while praying, Amy realized that when she planned to eventually move back to the States, she wasn't really settling in or truly investing in the friendships God sent her. By holding on to her desires, she was actually putting her needs, her wants, her*self* before God. When she ceased her campaign and submitted to God's authority over her life, she placed Him first.

Amy began referring to God's seasons of transitioning in her life as "holy disturbances." She practiced sharing her feelings with God honestly when she was in situations that she wanted to change. With Spirit-empowered contentment, she believed that whether God said, "Trust where I have you" or "Come away with me," He always had His children's best interests at heart.

Grateful for the husband and family she had asked for, Amy also thanked God for the experiences she couldn't have enjoyed if she'd stayed in America. She admitted that God had never let her down, even when she had grappled with trusting the path He had set before her. The Holy Spirit revealed how the love of Christ transformed her and her relationships with Him and others. By empowering her to yield to His authority, God gave her a testimony—her story—and enabled her to share Him with others.

In his letter to the church at Rome, the apostle Paul used his own testimony when speaking of this yielding of self to the Spirit of God. A continual spiritual warfare occurs in the life of a believer in Jesus who wants to live in step with the Holy Spirit. Paul wrote, "I know that good itself does not dwell in me, that is, in my sinful nature. For I have the desire to do what is good, but I cannot carry it out" (Romans 7:18).

The battle between our flesh and spirit is ongoing and unceasing, which means our dependence on the Holy Spirit must be intentional and continual. Paul declared, "I find this law at work: Although I want to do good, evil is right there with me. For in my inner being I delight in God's law; but I see another law at work in me, waging war against the law of my mind and making me a prisoner of the law of sin at work within me" (vv. 21–23).

Though this truth would seem to lead to hopelessness, Paul stood in confidence in his ability to live in victory through the power of the Holy Spirit even in times of trial. Admitting his own wretchedness, he affirmed, "Thanks be to God, who delivers me through Jesus Christ our Lord!" (v. 25). His use of the word *delivers* signifies a relentless act of liberation. Paul thanked God the Father for his salvation through God the Son, while acknowledging his complete and continual reliance on God the Spirit. Accepting the unchanging status of his sinful nature, Paul embraced his victorious freedom over sin sealed by his inalienable deliverance through Christ.

Paul identified a moment of spiritual warfare in which we choose rebellion and place ourselves above God in priority by living according to our flesh. He pointed out that "those who live according to the flesh have their minds set on what the flesh desires; but those who live in accordance with the Spirit have their minds set on what the Spirit desires" (Romans 8:5). Being tempted toward idolatry of self is not a sin. Giving in to temptations and choosing to please our flesh over pleasing God is the sin. Paul's words remind us that we have all we need to live in agreement with the Spirit and choose His way over our way. The Spirit enables us to follow Him when we submit to Him. Paul said, "If you live according to the flesh, you will die; but if by the Spirit you put to death the misdeeds of the body, you will live. For those who are led by the Spirit of God are the children of God" (Romans 8:13–14).

By intentionally deepening our personal relationship with Jesus, we demonstrate our desire to cease living for ourselves. We need not be perfect or get it right all the time to be obedient to God. By yielding to God's loving authority, we're simply placing ourselves under the lordship of Christ. When we ask the Holy Spirit to align our desires with God's desires, we can cease the campaigns of our flesh and submit our will to God's will, which is placing God first. In the power of the Holy Spirit, we can take each sacred stride on the path God sets before us from a position of worshipful surrender. We can remain faithful wherever He places us. Even when we don't get what we want, or when we're struggling after getting exactly what we asked for, we can trust that God will never let us down.

Inhale

Those who live according to the flesh have their minds set on what the flesh desires; but those who live in accordance with the Spirit have their minds set on what the Spirit desires. (Romans 8:5)

Exhale

Life-giving Spirit, thanks for loving us enough to reveal when our attitudes and actions are serving our sinful nature, pulling us from You, or damaging our relationships with You and others. Open our eyes to our actions and thoughts that hinder us from being content wherever You have us. Help us believe You will never let us down when our desires are aligned with Your heart. Empower us to cease our campaigns of the flesh and surrender to You as a love-motivated act of praise and obedience. In Jesus's name, amen.

SACRED STRIDE

Ask the Holy Spirit to determine what campaign of the flesh you need to cease so you can submit to His leading and God's Word.

9

Enduring Hope

STEP INTO GOD'S WORD
Romans 4:1–3, 18–21; 5:1–5

STAND ON GOD'S TRUTH
The Holy Spirit empowers us to release our
hopes and dreams into His loving hands.

As a tween, while her friends had begun sharing their interest in boys, Jennifer was making plans to serve God as a missionary doctor. Still, though she never dreamed of a fancy proposal or a big wedding, fifteen-year-old Jennifer wrote a list that described the man she would want to marry. Many items on that list reflected the traits she wanted to have too, the character traits of Jesus. Loving Jesus claimed the top spot on her list, which she tucked in her Bible and in her heart.

When Jennifer became a young adult, friends and some people in her church pressured her to date because they wanted her to be happy. She didn't understand their concerns because she was happy and content with where God had her. She didn't really desire the life others thought she needed.

However, during her late twenties, uncertainties stirred by

their comments and stemming from childhood trauma seeped into her thoughts. So as a new friendship with a young man grew, Jennifer asked God to reveal if marriage *was* part of His plan for her life. While others encouraged her to explore a relationship with her friend, Jennifer began to have feelings for him. His actions led her to believe he felt the same. Then, for the first time, Jennifer began dreaming of the possibility of marriage. Their friendship deepened over the years, increasing her hope. However, Jennifer began noticing some unhealthy patterns emerging. As she continued to pray, the Holy Spirit led her to walk away from the relationship. Though hurt and confused, she continued trusting that God knew what was best for her life.

While grieving the loss of such a close friendship and the death of an unexpected dream, Jennifer began to understand the pain of unreturned love. As she experienced the selfless love of God more intimately over the next three years, the Holy Spirit helped her discern when *she* failed to love God in return. Then, at the age of thirty, Jennifer entered a ten-year season of facing one closed door after another. She endured more personal hardships, including the loss of her family's business and her source of income. She began noticing that every time she tied her identity too closely to a dream, losing or letting go of that dream led to crisis.

Jennifer asked God to help her stop holding on to anything He wanted her to release and to walk into every promise He had intended for her. Sometimes, though, especially late at night, Jennifer's confidence wavered. She couldn't discern if she was listening to her own voice, the Enemy's voice, or the Holy Spirit's voice. She prayed, read her Bible, wrote in her journal, trusted God, and persevered in faith.

Two years later, while meeting with a small group of women

who made her feel comfortable enough to be vulnerable and transparent, Jennifer confessed the challenges of being single and over forty. As she continued prioritizing her relationship with God, though, Jennifer realized that she was more satisfied than ever in every aspect of life. The Holy Spirit helped her to embrace contentment in all seasons instead of worrying if she was missing out on something vital because of her singleness.

In the past, Jennifer would wonder if she had lost God's favor when she experienced hardship or had to release a dream. However, she discovered that His life-transforming mercies flowed abundantly when she simply believed God and surrendered to Him. As His love healed her heart one beat at a time, God affirmed her value as His daughter. He blessed her with new dreams, bigger dreams, dreams He had planned before she took her first breath of life.

God's people have always struggled to determine the source of their value, their ability to persevere in faith, and the stability of their hope. When the apostle Paul addressed the Christians in Rome, he established that Abraham was made right with God by faith alone—by trusting God, not by his own status or anything he had done or acquired (Romans 4:1–2). He said, "What does the Scripture say? Abraham believed God, and it was credited to him as righteousness" (v. 3). According to Paul, no one can boast about earning salvation. Likewise, no one needs to be afraid of losing salvation, because the gift of salvation is only received through believing in Christ.

Paul said, "Against all hope, Abraham in hope believed and so became the father of many nations, just as it had been said to him, 'So shall your offspring be'" (v. 18). Abraham didn't deny that he and his wife were past their childbearing years. "Yet he did not waver through unbelief regarding the promise of God, but was strengthened in his faith and gave glory to

God, being fully persuaded that God had power to do what he had promised" (vv. 19–21).

Abraham's heart-deep belief in God's power and authority became a testimony that would impact generations. Paul declared, "This is why 'it was credited to him as righteousness.' The words 'it was credited to him' were written not for him alone, but also for us, to whom God will credit righteousness— for us who believe in him who raised Jesus our Lord from the dead" (vv. 22–24).

Because, walking in Abraham's footsteps, we share in the things Paul said were true of our spiritual patriarch, "We have peace with God through our Lord Jesus Christ, through whom we have gained access by faith into this grace in which we now stand" (Romans 5:1–2). Christ's death on the cross tore the veil that separated us from God. When we received Christ as our personal Savior *and* submitted to Him as our Lord, we were welcomed into the holy of holies.

With God the Spirit *in* us, we now live in the very presence of God every moment of every day. We can navigate through life and rejoice in the glory of God's goodness and grace. "Not only so, but we also glory in our sufferings, because we know that suffering produces perseverance; perseverance, character; and character, hope. And hope does not put us to shame, because God's love has been poured out into our hearts through the Holy Spirit, who has been given to us" (vv. 3–5).

Sometimes we'll feel overcome by the tumultuous rogue waves of our circumstances. Sometimes we'll grow weary from treading water. We'll feel like sinking into a whirlpool of despair. But we will never, ever have to fight the rip currents of life on our own. When the winds of uncertainty wail, when problems pelt us from all sides, the Holy Spirit will enable us to walk by faith. So, we can dream big. We can experience the freedom of surrender with our hands, our hearts, and our minds open to what God deems is best for us. As we invite our loving Father to give and take away according to His good and perfect will, God the Spirit secures all our hope in God the Son.

Inhale

> Hope does not put us to shame, because God's love has been poured out into our hearts through the Holy Spirit, who has been given to us. (Romans 5:5)

Exhale

Hope-giving Spirit of God, thanks for reminding us that releasing dreams into Your loving hands is not letting dreams go or letting dreams die. Rather, our willingness to surrender our dreams to You is an act of worship that protects us from idolatry and leads us to the dreams You've intended for us all along. Uproot any dreams we've been clinging to or allowing others to force upon us through their expectations. Take away any dreams we've made idols. Please align our dreams with the God-given gifts and purpose You've planned for us, as we rejoice in the goodness of Your sanctifying mercies. In Jesus's name, amen.

SACRED STRIDE

Ask the Holy Spirit to uproot any dreams that are not in alignment with His plan for you and help you grieve those dreams. Then ask Him to empower you to embrace your value as God's beloved image-bearer, reveal the next sacred stride to move toward fulfilling your purpose-fueled dreams, and rest in His life-giving hope.

10

Commissioned to Love

STEP INTO GOD'S WORD
1 John 4:7–21

STAND ON GOD'S TRUTH
*The Holy Spirit leads us with love so that we can
love our neighbors wherever He leads us.*

Lucretia struggled to process her feelings in the aftermath
of yet another murder of an unarmed Black man, Trayvon
Martin—seventeen years old, just a *child*. She lamented and
embraced God's personal and missional work of racial healing,
a process designed to establish trust by closing the gaps of racial
division. Through the nurturing of genuine relationships, she
trusted God would create a safe space to share real and perceived
differences. She believed healing required telling the whole truth
about the past and acknowledging the historical and present
impact of individual, generational, and systemic racism. As
Lucretia had found, both in her studies and in her personal
life, racial healing allowed God's image-bearers to discover the

varying but very real physical, mental, emotional, and spiritual effect of racism on all people God created and loves.

She couldn't understand why God would want her to devote her studies to understanding race, a man-made social construct developed for oppression. Generations had been convinced that race and skin color determined the core of a person's identity and value as a human being. Lucretia had no idea how to deconstruct that falsehood. Teaching anti-racism sounded too big—how could she possibly make a difference? But she wanted to obey God, so she accepted His charge.

Often overwhelmed by the work involved in racial healing, Lucretia prayed. God helped her realize that she only had to do one thing: *her* thing. One drop would cause a ripple effect. And Lucretia believed that, through the power of the Spirit of God in her, she could do one drop.

In 1997, during a trip to Africa, God took her on a very specific journey to learn what race and anti-racism meant. Lucretia prayerfully established a four-step process that paralleled spiritual growth and became the foundation for all her work: "From *education* comes *revelation* that empowers *transformation* and leads to *liberation*."

She leaned into the apostle Paul's teaching: "Do not conform to the pattern of this world, but be transformed by the renewing of your mind. Then you will be able to test and approve what God's will is—his good, pleasing and perfect will" (Romans 12:2). Lucretia recognized race and racism were patterns of this world that were created by man to distort the identities of God's image-bearers. As she studied the Bible, she discovered her core identity in Christ and began to walk in that truth. Her work in racial healing taught her more about God and the people He created and loves. When she got married, that work became even more personal.

She and her husband knew people would ask their children, "*What* are you?" They wanted to prepare them to answer with confidence in *who* they were as God's image-bearers. One day their four-year-old daughter gave them the language they needed. The little girl didn't see her parents as a White man married to a Black woman; she saw her family as people with different shades of brown skin. Lucretia and her husband taught their daughter about melanin and her family's African and European ancestors. They encouraged her to explore and express her feelings when faced with the history of racism.

As God grew their family in size, they all got more comfortable in their skin. Through their honest and sometimes heartbreaking conversations, the Holy Spirit inspired Lucretia to share with others all that God was teaching her. She created accessible, scholarly informed, evidence-based anti-racism educational resources.

After the Charleston, South Carolina, church massacre in 2015, Lucretia's multiracial church family reached out and asked her for help. Together, they created a safe space where people were free to ask questions and heal emotionally.

People are accustomed to sharing opinions and experiences, which are valid. However, Lucretia taught that learning leads to understanding that helps each person become part of the solutions. She began creating more resources to equip both younger and older learners with the language and confidence to discuss phenotype, culture, ethnicity, and race. Soon her biblical worldview became welcomed in spaces that were not affiliated with Christianity.

When Lucretia grew weary and discouraged by opposition to her teaching, especially in the church, God rejuvenated her with testimonies. The Holy Spirit was making changes that crossed generational, cultural, and international lines inside and outside the church, as people were becoming drops that caused widening ripples of love.

In 1 John 4:7–8, the apostle John provided a simple call to action: "Dear friends, let us love one another, for love comes from God. Everyone who loves has been born of God and knows God. Whoever does not love does not know God, because God is love." God the Father demonstrated His love for us through God the Son, whose sacrifice on the cross served as an atonement for our sins (vv. 9–10). John said, "Since God so loved us, we also ought to love one another. No one has ever seen God; but if we love one another, God lives in us and his love is made complete in us" (vv. 11–12). Selfless and sacrificial love in action goes against the patterns of this world. When others see this Christlike love in us, we can point them to Jesus through authentic, healthy, and holy relationships.

The apostle John said, "This is how love is made complete among us so that we will have confidence on the day of judgment: In this world we are like Jesus" (v. 17). Being an ambassador for Christ may feel impossible due to our sin nature. However, all believers in Jesus have complete and continual access to the Holy Spirit's power. "We love because he first loved us" (v. 19). We can love because He empowers us to love, because He is loving, and because He *is* love.

Truly loving one another as neighbors, however, entails accurately seeing and hearing each other, learning from and empathizing with each other, relating to and growing with each other. Love demands that we eradicate "us-and-them" from our vocabulary and our thinking. Loving our neighbors requires believing God made all people and loves all people, even those who reject Him. Jesus-Love demands the willingness to die to self for the sake of another, to understand that when sin hurts one person, *all* the people God made and loves are hurt.

Though one person cannot change the entire world, we can each do one thing: *our* thing. We can each be a drop that causes ripple effects of Jesus-Love within our small spheres of influence. Through the biblically based teaching of anti-racism, the Holy Spirit can transform us and prepare us to fulfill our individual and communal purposes within God's beautifully diverse kingdom. He empowers us to make disciples of all nations—the Great Commission—by loving God and others—the Greatest Commandment. Simply put, that just means we are commissioned to love all the people God made and loves.

Inhale

[Jesus] has given us this command: Anyone who loves God must also love their brother and sister. (1 John 4:21)

Exhale

Life-transforming Spirit of God, thanks for securing us in Your unconditional love. Continue opening our hearts and minds so we can recognize and repent of our personal biases and prejudices, both unintentional and intentional. Empower us with the courage to forgive one another and celebrate the value of all Your image-bearers as we stand together against injustice, inequality, marginalization, oppression, and racism. Reveal our "one thing" so we can each be a drop, causing ripple effects of Jesus-Love around the world. Help us honor You with the work of racial healing for Your glory and the advancement of Your beautifully diverse kingdom. In Jesus's name, amen.

SACRED STRIDE

Ask the Holy Spirit to help you fulfill your commission to love all people as you prayerfully work toward racial healing, demonstrated with your words, actions, and attitudes.

11

Better Together

STEP INTO GOD'S WORD
1 Corinthians 12:12–31

STAND ON GOD'S TRUTH
*The Holy Spirit values every person because
every person is made in God's image.*

After only a month at home with her newborn son, Row, Caroline began to suspect his vision impairment. A few weeks later, doctors diagnosed Row with congenital eye disease. Caroline tried to be strong and positive. She tried to trust God as she mourned the loss of the life she had dreamed Row would experience. But she didn't know how to help him when he screamed. Sobbing and lamenting, she realized that she just wasn't strong enough.

In her desperation, she asked for prayer support from the women in her Bible study group and began seeking God in the Scriptures. As she prayed, the Holy Spirit began using her journal entries to bring Caroline peace. He showed her how He was using Row in her life to help her grow.

Caroline began noticing how her toddlers interacted. Though

Tripp helped his brother when needed, he played with Row as if his disability didn't matter. The Holy Spirit showed her that children with and without disabilities could build genuine relationships when given opportunities to get to know each other.

In 2020, after Row turned two, a woman in Caroline's Bible study group announced she was pregnant with twins. Caroline began praying for her. After Francie gave birth to Hall and Barrett, the group received another prayer request. Hall was born with Down syndrome.

As Francie visited Hall in the neonatal intensive care unit, her frustration rose. Although her husband and their extended family embraced both of her sons immediately, Francie found it difficult to bond with Hall. Having never been around people with disabilities, she feared the unknowns and worried about the future.

Her family encouraged her, affirmed their love for her and the twins, and committed to learning more about Down syndrome together. Still, Francie grieved over the life she'd imagined for her boys. As she read her Bible, prayed, journaled, and worked with a life coach, the Holy Spirit gave her everything she needed to get through each day. Trusting Him was hard. But as she drew nearer to God, Francie began seeing Hall as her "grade-A baby"—top notch and of the highest quality. She thanked God for helping her realize that He had created both of her sons in His image, and for using Hall to make *her* a better person.

In October 2020 Caroline reached out to Francie. She shared her dream of starting a nonprofit to help children embrace differences and build relationships through intentional kindness. Both women wanted to help others gain the confidence to include, celebrate, and love all God's image-bearers. They prayed, planned, and founded a nonprofit that invited communities to become more inclusive while nurturing loving relationships between people with and without disabilities. And in November 2020, they began using my picture book *Different Like Me* as a part of their curriculum.

Caroline admitted that before God blessed her family with Row, Tripp's library didn't include books that showed people who were different from them. She and Francie wanted to ensure other children could enjoy books that celebrated diversity and inclusion while increasing disability awareness. They decided to give away one free book per child during their events. However, creating a book list that introduced diverse human characters and included children with different disabilities proved challenging. The greater challenge became finding books that honored Jesus by aligning with their Christian values and that public schools would accept.

As God provided, He expanded Caroline and Francie's vision for the ministry. They began featuring other families on their website and social media pages. They prayed God would use this exposure to help create safe spaces for adults and children to ask questions. Testimonies from supporters affirmed that God was helping people through their work. And as God connected them with more volunteers, schools, a board of directors, authors, and supporters online and in their local community, He proved that their diverse team worked better together.

In 1 Corinthians 12, the apostle Paul said there are "different kinds of gifts, but the same Spirit distributes them" and "different kinds of service, but the same Lord" (vv. 4–5). He continued, "There are different kinds of working, but in all of them and in everyone it is the same God at work" (v. 6). Paul listed some of the gifts endowed by the Holy Spirit. He acknowledged the talents, skills, abilities, and experiences that make us unique and prepared for service in His kingdom, then shifted the focus back to the people made in God's image. "Just as a body, though one, has many parts, but all its many parts form one body, so it is with Christ," Paul wrote (v. 12). He expressed the value and necessity of diversity in the body of Christ, the church, which is God's kingdom (vv. 15–20). Every person, said Paul, fills a unique and God-ordained role: "In fact God has placed the parts in the body, every one of them, just as he wanted them to be" (v. 18).

Paul urged the Corinthians to recognize how essential every part of the body is to the whole; in fact, "those parts of the body that seem to be weaker are indispensable" (vv. 21–22). Every person matters and makes a difference in God's kingdom. Our various gifts add even more value when we work together. More importantly, all people are gifts simply because we exist, because God created us in His image *on* purpose and *with* a purpose.

"God has put the body together," said the apostle, "giving greater honor to the parts that lacked it, so that there should be no division in the body, but that its parts should have equal concern for each other" (vv. 24–25). Row, Hall, and Tripp are examples of this truth in action. These young boys didn't do anything but be themselves, as God intentionally created them to be. Yet, over time, the Holy Spirit used them to transform their mothers and inspire their communities to nurture loving relationships through intentional kindness.

As we live and love within the beautifully diverse communities God created and loves, the Holy Spirit can use all of us to refine and encourage one another, as we work together to reach more people with the gospel of Jesus Christ. Confirming the depth of connection in the living body of Christ, Paul said, "If one part suffers, every part suffers with it; if one part is honored, every part rejoices with it" (v. 26). When we consider our interdependence as God's children, we begin to recognize inclusion and kindness toward others as God-honoring self-care *and* missional work in the name of Jesus.

To the church then and now, Paul confirmed that our diversity within our unity is essential to God's plan. He said, "Now you are the body of Christ, and each one of you is a part of it" (v. 27). We are responsible for one another. We need one another. Partnering with the Holy Spirit, we can demonstrate that each person is an invaluable member of God's kingdom by getting comfortable with our differences. When we spend time serving each other with kindness, the Spirit will help us get to truly know, understand, and love others as Jesus loves us. As He works in and through each of us, He will expand His kingdom and prove we are simply better together.

Inhale

Now you are the body of Christ, and each one of you is a part of it. (1 Corinthians 12:27)

Exhale

Compassionate Spirit, thanks for placing us in the right spaces at the right times. Thanks for making divine plans that connect us with others You value and love just like us. Thanks for working in and through our lives and the lives of those You choose to use to make us more like Jesus. Please forgive us when we avoid people who make us feel uncomfortable because they are different from us. Give us courage to be intentionally kind as we make our personal spaces more diverse by investing in loving fellowship and genuine relationship building with You and others. In Jesus's name, amen.

SACRED STRIDE

Ask the Holy Spirit to give you opportunities to be kind to all people who are different from you. Take a few more sacred strides by asking Him for ways you can learn about and enhance disability awareness. How can you develop authentic and supportive relationships with people who are disabled or with families with disabled children?

12

Forever Changing

STEP INTO GOD'S WORD
Acts 9:1–31

STAND ON GOD'S TRUTH
The Holy Spirit transforms us immediately and day by day.

In December 2001, I told my mom I had become a Christian. The first thing out of her mouth was, "Don't judge me or try to change me."

I assured her I had no business judging anyone. Then I said, "I can't even change myself. That's God's job, not mine." I spent the next seven and a half months trying to show my mom the love of Jesus during our daily calls. Then in the summer of 2002, I messed up. Big time!

After setting up my classroom for my first vacation Bible school, I realized I had left my costume and some supplies in a box on my dining room table. I left Xavier at the church with his VBS group leader and rushed out the door. Soon groups of children would be expecting me to teach them about Jesus.

Grateful that we only lived a few minutes from our church, I sinned past the speed limit signs and asked forgiveness along the way. I raced into the house, grabbed the box, and barreled out the door. My parents, and my aunt and uncle who lived over an hour away, pulled up to the curb.

Extremely aware of the seconds ticking away as my mom walked toward me, I said, "I'm on my way to church for an event. Why didn't you call first?"

My mom told everyone to get back into the car. They left without looking back.

I sped down the street, cursing and complaining about my mom's attitude. I did not ask for forgiveness as I drove toward the church . . . where I would be teaching children about Jesus. When I got stuck behind a red light, I got madder. Then, I laughed at the audacity of my hypocrisy and begged God for forgiveness.

I stepped into the sanctuary, just in time to slip into my costume and invite the first group of children into my class-room. We had a wonderful night learning how Jesus loved us and commanded us to love Him and others. After we got home, I called my mom to apologize.

She refused to get on the phone with me.

Though I reached out multiple times a day during their weeklong visit to California, she went home without speaking to me or seeing my family. Over the next few months, I left apologies on her answering machine. Sometimes I ranted about her "being ridiculous." Then I called to apologize for my rants.

Finally, I surrendered to what the Holy Spirit had been nudging me to do all along. I trusted Him to work as I prayed for my mom daily. I called once a week to say "I love you" to her answering machine or to pass the message through my dad. I sent cards and gifts for holidays. She communicated with my husband and sons but didn't speak to me for an entire year.

When my parents returned for their yearly trip the following summer, my mom promised my husband that she would meet with me. I drove to my aunt and uncle's house with my friend Cendy and our sons. When we arrived, my cousin said our parents had left earlier that morning. Though my anger initially rose, the Holy Spirit caused me to pause.

Cendy and I took the boys to the creek behind the house, caught crawdads, and picked plump blackberries. As I prayed and breathed in the country air, the Holy Spirit and my friend encouraged me to extend grace, forgiveness, and love toward my mom. I prayed silently as we enjoyed the rest of the day. The details of the conflict with my mom didn't matter as much when the Spirit of God revealed my greatest offense. I had messed up my chance to be a witness for Jesus by putting *going* to church above *being* the loving church.

Before we left, I wrote my mom a note. I apologized for my actions and my attitude. I told her that I loved her and missed our daily chats. And I promised to keep praying for *us*.

The next day my mom called and said, "You've changed."

That was the first of our many conversations about Jesus.

A year later, my mom accepted Christ as her personal Savior and Lord. She prayed for our family daily. We resumed our morning calls and praised God for the ways He was changing us. After doctors diagnosed her with leukemia in January 2014, I bought an airline ticket so I could stay with her in the ICU. As the monitors beeped in the dark room, I asked God to give me a sign that she truly accepted Christ as her Savior.

Without opening her eyes, my mom reached for me. I held her hand and leaned in to hear her whisper, "I feel God with me. May His will be done. I am at peace." After she was released, I asked her about that night. She didn't even remember speaking to me. But I knew the Holy Spirit had spoken through her.

My mom asked me to be her live-in caregiver when she started treatment in June. I didn't know if I would be able to help her. My back injury caused chronic nerve pain, severe muscle spasms, and debilitating headaches. Sometimes, I could barely get out of bed. After I shared my concerns with my husband, we decided I should go after our son's birthday in July.

Before I left for Seattle, God led my doctors to provide a treatment plan to help manage my pain. I woke at five every morning to take my first dose of medication so my mom wouldn't see me hunched over when our day started an hour later. At one point during my stay, one wrong step had me using crutches for six weeks, which increased my upper back pain. I prayed every day, asking God to be my strength and my peace one sacred stride at a time. He sent some to help us while others encouraged us by sending cards that we taped on the wall as reminders of His love and care. And God blessed me with the pleasure and privilege of serving my mom for four months. I prayed at her side in October that same year, when my mom—my sister in Christ—took her last breath and Jesus welcomed her home.

Though I miss her and am in tears as I write these words, I do not grieve "like the rest of mankind, who have no hope" (1 Thessalonians 4:13). As God continues comforting me, He is also working on me and making me more like Jesus each day. He uses Scripture to assure me that my mom immediately joined Jesus in eternity. "For we believe that Jesus died and rose again, and so we believe that God will bring with Jesus those who have fallen asleep in him" (v. 14).

When I want to call my mom, just to hear her voice, the Holy Spirit comforts me with the promise of Christ's return in power and glory, and of the resurrection. "The Lord himself will come down from heaven, with a loud command, with the voice of the archangel and with the trumpet call of God, and the dead in Christ will rise first. After that, we who are still alive and are left will be caught up together with them in the clouds to meet the Lord in the air. And so we will be with the Lord forever" (1 Thessalonians 4:16–17). Until then, I thank God for every opportunity to share the good news that changed my life, my mom's life, and our relationship with each other and with Him forever.

God loves every person in this world and thinks we're all worth pursuing. Every life changed by the love of Christ is a miracle of His mercy that the Holy Spirit can use to draw others into the Father's embrace. The Bible says Jesus was pursuing Saul while he "was still breathing out murderous threats against the Lord's disciples" (Acts 9:1). As Saul searched for Christ followers to imprison, he heard Jesus calling him by name (vv. 2–4). God the Son identified Himself to Saul: "'I am Jesus, whom you are persecuting,' he replied. 'Now get up and go into the city, and you will be told what you must do'" (vv. 5–6). Saul "got up from the ground," blinded and dependent on others to lead him to the place Jesus directed him to go (vv. 7–9). Saul wasn't too far for God to reach. He wasn't too messed up, and he didn't mess up too much for God to love, save, change, and use for His glory to advance His kingdom.

At that time, Jesus called another man by name, "a disciple named Ananias" (v. 10). Ananias responded without hesitation, though he confessed to fearing Saul's reputation and doubting the Lord could use such a man (vv. 10–14). "But the Lord said to Ananias, 'Go! This man is my chosen instrument to proclaim my name to the Gentiles and their kings and to the people of Israel'" (v. 15). Jesus would use Saul but also promised his journey would include suffering.

Ananias embraced Saul as a brother in the faith and witnessed Saul's changed life firsthand (vv. 17–19). Saul began preaching in the power of the Spirit, astonishing listeners by proclaiming and "proving that Jesus is the Messiah" (vv. 20–22). He escaped death and endured rejection by fellow believers (vv. 23–26). But the Holy Spirit supported Saul as he continued "speaking boldly in the name of the Lord" and leading others to Jesus (vv. 27–30). In the wake of Saul's life-changing experience on the road to Damascus, his witness caused waves of faith-building testimonies. "Then the church throughout Judea, Galilee and Samaria enjoyed a time of peace and was strengthened. Living in the fear of the Lord and encouraged by the Holy Spirit, it increased in numbers" (v. 31).

We may not always be able to see how the Holy Spirit uses our journey of immediate and continual transformation. He often makes His presence known through our small acts of kindness and our selfless love and service to those in need. However, God can also expand His kingdom when others watch us fall short, repent, seek forgiveness, and submit to His authority with love-motivated obedience. When others can see how the Holy Spirit has changed us and witness His ongoing work of transformation in us, He draws their attention to the unchanging Messiah, Jesus. As we submit to God the Spirit one sacred stride at a time, we become the forever-changing testimonies that honor God the Father by pointing to the never-changing love of God the Son.

Inhale

Immediately, something like scales fell from Saul's eyes, and he could see again. He got up and was baptized, and after taking some food, he regained his strength. (Acts 9:18–19)

Exhale

Spirit of God, please empower us to recognize and repent from our sins as we submit to Your authority and life-transforming love. Please use our testimonies to point others to a saving relationship with Jesus. Thank You for being patient with us and for pursuing us relentlessly. You are the only one who can change hearts and renew minds. So please change us so we can love others enough to share Your word while You do Your holy work of changing us and them. In Jesus's name, amen.

SACRED STRIDE

Ask the Holy Spirit to reveal specific ways He has changed the way you think, believe, and behave since the day you first received Jesus as your Savior and Lord. Then ask Him to reveal how He wants to change you now, as you pray for those who have not yet received Christ.

13

Always at Home

STEP INTO GOD'S WORD
Romans 15:1–13

STAND ON GOD'S TRUTH
*When we're at home in the Spirit's presence,
others feel at home in our presence.*

Born and raised in a Christian home in India, a country where less than 5 percent of the population follows Jesus, Mabel understood how to live in a countercultural way. Still, even living as a minority in India couldn't prepare her for the struggles that awaited her when she married Simon and moved to America at the age of thirty. With her husband working long hours, Mabel became homesick. As she struggled to find a place to fit in and to belong, she battled loneliness, depression, and feelings of abandonment and resentment.

In India, Mabel spoke English, learned about Western culture, and remained active in her church and community. In America, over their decade of moving from place to place, she didn't feel at home in any of the ten neighborhoods or seven cities in which they'd lived. Some people treated her rudely and said cruel things when they became impatient with her accent or intolerant of her cultural differences. But Mabel loved Jesus and people. She wanted to honor God and represent Him well. So she prayed for the people who were unkind to her and tried to be kind and friendly in response.

Still, Mabel couldn't understand why some people didn't accept her. She came to question her identity and self-worth and, as a result, her relationship with God and what He was doing in her life.

When her husband's job led them to California, God connected them with a new Bible study group. The Holy Spirit used this loving community to revive Mabel's hope and revitalize her faith.

One day, on their way home from an event, Mabel and her husband were in a car accident. Two couples from the church they had visited cared for Mabel and Simon during their recovery. These people's willingness to serve God by sacrificing their time and resources for near strangers humbled Mabel. Her prayers began to change. She no longer thrust self-focused requests at God. Instead, she began to pray for and serve others generously.

As quickly as the Spirit built Mabel's hope, though, God drew them through not just one but two short-order moves—first to Arkansas during the second trimester of Mabel's first pregnancy, then back to India for the birth of their son, Ryan.

Once Mabel was surrounded by family and friends who loved her, her faith began to thrive again. But her respite didn't last long. Her husband's job required them to move back to America.

Living so far away from her supportive family and friends as a new mom proved harder for Mabel than any other relocation. Desperate to avoid her previous trials, she determined to find a

Bible study as soon as her family settled into their new home. As she opened herself up for fellowship and prayed for God's provision, the Holy Spirit revealed that her primary relationship could not be with her husband, her family, or her friends. Mabel began spending more time with God, not to check Bible reading off her task list but to know God and connect with Him. The Holy Spirit helped her realize that where she lived wasn't the problem. Wherever she called home, being accepted or finding the right church could not satisfy the needs of her soul.

Eventually God led Mabel's family to a loving, Bible-teaching church. He gave them opportunities to serve immigrants transitioning from India to America. Mabel's experiences and personal struggles equipped her to share how God could work in their lives, just as He was working in her life. As Mabel served others, God continued His healing work in her.

The Holy Spirit confirmed that Mabel's identity and worth were not based on any job or accomplishment, on any title or status, or on her current address. God reminded her that all believers are foreigners on this earth, designed to live as spiritual immigrants. Mabel could no longer live as if this earth were her home. Rejoicing in this revelation, she wrote a book and began sharing what God was teaching her. As the Holy Spirit helped Mabel feel at home in the peace of His presence, He enabled her to help others feel more at home in her presence.

In the Bible, God spoke through Moses: "When a foreigner resides among you in your land, do not mistreat them. The foreigner residing among you must be treated as your native-born. Love them as yourself, for you were foreigners in Egypt. I am the LORD your God" (Leviticus 19:33–34). Though God spoke specifically to the Israelites in that moment in history, the Scriptures support that God consistently taught His followers to love foreigners, all of which He considers our neighbors. Though the common definition of *foreigners* is "immigrants" or "refugees"—people from a different country or culture—to be a foreigner simply means being a newcomer, a stranger or a sojourner. Someone who is different.

While in Corinth, the apostle Paul wrote a letter to the Christians in Rome who had a tough time accepting the gentiles. He said, "Each of us should please our neighbors for their good, to build them up. For even Christ did not please himself" (Romans 15:2–3). He spoke a prayer of blessing and holy commission over the church: "May the God who gives endurance and encouragement give you the same attitude of mind toward each other that Christ Jesus had, so that with one mind and one voice you may glorify the God and Father of our Lord Jesus Christ" (vv. 5–6). With this charge, Paul called believers to accept each other just as Jesus had accepted them (v. 7).

Paul challenged the believers to honor God's plan, which He made from the beginning, and welcome the gentiles into God's family for His glory (vv. 8–11). He quoted Isaiah 11:10, which includes multiple nations: "'The Root of Jesse will spring up, one who will arise to rule over the nations; in him the Gentiles will hope'" (Romans 15:12). In his final blessing, the apostle said, "May the God of hope fill you with all joy and peace as you trust in him, so that you may overflow with hope by the power of the Holy Spirit" (v. 13).

As Christ loves us, the Spirit will surely enable us to love other foreigners and share Him with those who do not yet accept Christ as Lord. Through the Spirit we can live in the freedom of our citizenship in heaven, which sets us all apart as foreigners on this earth. God remains with us wherever we go. From that unchangeable foundation of security and its surplus of hope, we can feel at home in the Holy Spirit's presence and make others feel at home in our presence.

Inhale

Accept one another, then, just as Christ accepted you, in order to bring praise to God. (Romans 15:7)

Exhale

Welcoming Spirit of God, thanks for making us feel at home wherever we are, for You are there with us. Grow us as we serve You together as citizens of heaven. When we have treated others poorly or made Your beloved image-bearers feel unwelcome, lead us to repent and seek forgiveness. When people have treated us or people we love poorly because of differences, empower us to forgive them. Please help us see and love newcomers and those who might feel alone, invisible, or excluded, as we nurture authentic, loving, and respectful relationships with others made in Your image. In Jesus's name, amen.

SACRED STRIDE

Ask the Holy Spirit to be your comfort when you feel out of place or far from home. Ask Him to reveal when you've made others feel out of place or unwelcome, even if you've done so unintentionally. Then ask Him to show you practical ways you can serve and love people who are different from you, especially the immigrants, refugees, and foreigners He places in your path.

14

Love Ever Flowing

STEP INTO GOD'S WORD
Galatians 5:22–23; 1 John 4:7–21

STAND ON GOD'S TRUTH
*The Holy Spirit empowers us to love exceedingly
from the ever-flowing well of His love for us.*

In 2001, Shawn met Dorina on a missionary trip to Haiti. He encouraged his friend Ericlee to date her. Two years later Shawn prayed over the couple during their wedding. The three friends continued serving Jesus and supporting one another after Shawn moved across the country.

In 2012, Shawn's pastor shared a message that moved him and God placed widows on his heart. Shawn asked Ericlee and Dorina to pray for discernment as he considered returning to California so he could support a widow he loved deeply—his mom. Two years later, Shawn applied for a job in California and received an invitation to interview. However, before Shawn could meet with his potential employer, Ericlee died from cancer. While grieving the loss of his good friend and shortly before driving to his funeral, Shawn completed that interview. The following weekend he dedicated his Ironman Triathlon to Ericlee.

As Dorina grieved and helped her three daughters process the tragic loss of their father, Shawn's gesture lifted her heavy heart. The Holy Spirit nudged her to call and thank her friend. They talked about celebrating Ericlee's life as they wept over their loss.

Shawn wanted to support the couple's daughters, whom he'd come to love over the years. He took them to a pumpkin patch event at their church and shared stories about his good friend.

When her mother encouraged her to believe God had someone else for her to love, Dorina rejected the possibility. However, she soon began wondering if Shawn could be that someone. Lamenting over her broken love story and the weight of mothering three little girls, she released her sorrow in heart-wrenching prayers. The Spirit comforted her as she wrestled with confusing and quickly growing feelings for Shawn.

Meanwhile, Shawn had asked people to pray as he processed *his* unexpected and changing feelings toward Dorina. Others affirmed the couple before they even shared their feelings with each other. They both held back and prayed, stepping cautiously with the Holy Spirit's nudging to move forward in their relationship.

As she prayed, Dorina realized a relationship with Shawn wasn't God's plan B for her. Their relationship was simply the next chapter of her love story. In God's perfect timing, nervous but confident, Dorina took one sacred stride toward the man she believed her late husband would have entrusted to care for his family.

Shawn believed God had assigned Ericlee to love and care for Dorina and the girls for the first half of their story, and now God had sent him to love and care for them going forward.

When the couple finally shared their feelings with one another, they prayed together and allowed everyone space to grieve and heal. Then, in 2016, the girls stood with the couple at their wedding. As Shawn embraced Dorina as his beloved bride and the girls as his beloved daughters, the girls grew to consider him as their loving father.

Like most couples, Shawn and Dorina celebrated their anniversary each year. However, the family also committed to hosting a yearly "heaven-iversary" party. They invited family and friends to celebrate Ericlee's life of love for God and others. And in December 2022, when Shawn officially adopted all three girls, they honored *and* included the memory of Ericlee.

The Holy Spirit led Dorina to share their story and God's Word. The couple wrote a devotional together. The family hosted a podcast. Dorina writes Bible studies and even went back to writing children's books, something she had enjoyed doing before she became a widow. Trusting the Holy Spirit, who enables them to draw from His endless supply of love, the family serves God together and is able to love each other and others exceedingly and abundantly more that they dreamed possible.

Love is the surefire earmark of a Christ follower. The disciple John* wrote, "Dear friends, let us love one another, for love comes from God. Everyone who loves has been born of God and knows God. Whoever does not love does not know God, because God is love" (1 John 4:7–8).

John continues, "This is how God showed his love among us: He sent his one and only Son into the world that we might live through him. This is love: not that we loved God, but that he loved us and sent his Son as an atoning sacrifice for our sins"

---

* John is commonly understood to be "the disciple whom Jesus loved" (John 13:23). Who better to write about love than the apostle closest to the Lord's heart?

(vv. 9–10). John insists that our ability to love has its source in Jesus's sacrificial, selfless, unconditional, and everlasting love for us. God's love never runs out or expires. And love cannot be excluded from our relationships with God or people.

The apostle proclaimed, "This is how we know that we live in him and he in us: He has given us of his Spirit" (v. 13). With a refreshing sense of simplicity and practicality to his teaching, John takes the focus off self and points to the Holy Spirit, the one who gives us all we need to love. John declared, "God *is* love. Whoever lives in love lives in God, and God in them" (vv. 15–16, emphasis mine). This love goes beyond our words and into our actions and attitudes, our testimonies and love stories.

God's love is unconditional, intimate, and sacrificial. His selfless, costly, and ever-flowing love for us empowers us to love (v. 19). His love changes everything and should change the way we relate to Him and others. God's unconditional love transforms our view of who we are and our perception of our value. The security of God's love fuels our compassion, confidence, and courage. This impacts how we navigate through life, how we relate to others, and how we see others and respond to their love extended toward us.

John teaches us to take love seriously and personally. "Whoever claims to love God yet hates a brother or sister is a liar. For whoever does not love their brother and sister, whom they have seen, cannot love God, whom they have not seen. And he has given us this command: Anyone who loves God must also love their brother and sister" (1 John 4:20–21). Love for one another isn't an option; it's both the outflow and the proof of our love of God.

If we love God, grief cannot squelch our love for others. Resentment, bitterness, anger, or fear cannot hinder our God-given capacity to love. Though we may need time to process emotions as God mends our broken hearts, nothing can limit the depth of love we can have for others . . . *if* we love God. Because He loved us first. He's the initiator. The Holy Spirit, whose fruit *is* love, provides all we need to love unconditionally, exceedingly and abundantly more than we can dream possible.

Inhale

> We love because he first loved us. (1 John 4:19)

Exhale

Loving Spirit of God, thanks for reviving us with the power of Your ever-flowing love for us. Help us love You and others from the unending love supply You give us. Thanks for reminding us that You will never stop loving us, even when we struggle to love well or are afraid to love again. Tear away anything hindering us from recognizing and receiving love from You and others. Please give us grateful hearts that overflow with loving obedience to Your commands as we fall deeper in love with You each day. In Jesus's name, amen.

SACRED STRIDE

Consider the ways God has shown His love for you and helped you love others with your words, actions, and attitudes. How can you show love to others today?

15

Joy Is Now and Forever

STEP INTO GOD'S WORD
Psalm 100

STAND ON GOD'S TRUTH
The Holy Spirit is our source of joy as we live in the present with an eternal perspective.

For ten years, Randy and Cheri went through numerous fertility treatments. Randy had only two requests for God. He prayed, "Please don't give me a child that will not have eternity with You. And don't give me a disabled child, since I won't be able to bear it." Though the waiting was long and hard, Randy believed God would answer his prayers. He began making plans for his child. And at the age of forty-three, Cheri announced her pregnancy.

Everything seemed perfect during the pregnancy, and labor went well . . . until doctors delivered CJ and whisked him away from his parents without explanation. While it hadn't been diagnosed in utero, God had given them a child with Down syndrome.

Cheri quickly adjusted and began learning how to care for their son's special needs. But the diagnosis crushed Randy. He put the dreams he had for his son to death on the day of his birth.

The couple's Christian friends prayed over Randy in the hospital and over the next few months. Still, Randy grappled with his feelings as he struggled to bond with his son. He cried out to God. Then when CJ was six months old, Randy accepted that God's plan was just *different* from his plan. He couldn't explain what happened inside him or how everything changed. One day he simply loved his son exactly as God had created him. And over time, as he grew closer to God and CJ, Randy learned that a diagnosis did not have to be a limitation or the end of his dreams for his son.

The couple did all they could to equip their son to be independent and raised him to know, love, and serve God. In 2018, to increase CJ's independence, they sent him to school alone for the first time. After school, Cheri waited in front of their home while fourteen-year-old CJ exited the school bus. As he walked down the long driveway and started dancing, Cheri pulled out her phone and caught him on video. From that day on, she recorded CJ's after-school dance show and shared the clips with family and friends.

One day, Cheri shared her story with the men who picked up their trash each week. The two men walked to the end of the driveway, met CJ when he got off the bus, and boogied with him all the way home. Cheri posted the video online, and God used CJ and his new friends to spread joy throughout their entire community and beyond.

The next year, during a lonely day in our new home in

Wisconsin, the Holy Spirit encouraged *me* as I watched the video of CJ dancing with the two men. I wrote about him in an *Our Daily Bread* devotion, "Our Reason for Joy." God used that devotion, published over a year later on June 9, 2020, to point readers around the world to God—the only lasting source of true joy. And Cheri, alerted to my article by a friend, reached out to thank me. God had answered their prayers and used their son to bless others for Jesus through this unexpected international ministry opportunity. CJ's devotional story has since been published in multiple languages and distributed to millions of people around the world. Still, CJ's greatest impact has been at home, especially in the life of his father.

CJ reads the Bible and prays with his family. He loves God and has accepted Jesus as his Savior and Lord. Thankful that God said yes to his first prayer, Randy praises God for saying no to his second. No longer focusing on his son's disabilities, he celebrates CJ, the child God created and entrusted to him.

In 2020, to help with speech therapy, Randy and Cheri started recording CJ giving local weather reports. With his parents encouraging him in the background, "The Weatherman Extraordinaire" told listeners the temperatures they could expect. He ends each episode with his signature dance moves and thumbs-up sign-off, spreading joy wherever God leads.

Though people have told Randy and Cheri that CJ is blessed to have them as parents, the couple insists that God blessed *them* with CJ. As they rely on the Holy Spirit when facing challenges and uncertainties, the family continues to grow closer to God and each other while serving Him with contagious joy.

Of all the persons in Scripture, the psalmist David had one of the most vibrant legacies of joy-filled faith anchored by his intimacy with God. He invited God's people to join him in singing praises to the Lord with jubilation. With contagious elation, David sang, "Shout for joy to the LORD, all the earth. Worship the LORD with gladness; come before him with joyful songs" (Psalm 100:1–2).

Motivated by love and gratitude, not obligation or duty, David worshiped God. He urged others to join him and to enter God's presence, to rejoice and acknowledge Him as creator and sustainer of all. David said, "Know that the LORD is God. It is he who made us, and we are his; we are his people, the sheep of his pasture" (v. 3). With this beautiful image of God's loving care, David called God's people to celebrate the gift of intimacy with the Shepherd who provides for and protects His beloved sheep. He knows and cares for us each by name, completely and personally.

Approaching God with exaltation and adoration, David said, "Enter his gates with thanksgiving and his courts with praise; give thanks to him and praise his name. For the LORD is good and his love endures forever; his faithfulness continues through all generations" (vv. 4–5). David's lifestyle of grateful praise and worship didn't depend on his circumstances nor on his ability or failure to follow God perfectly. His focus was not on himself. It was God whom David declared worthy of praise because of who He is and always will be.

Our lives may not go as planned. God may not answer our prayers as we hoped. Still, we can trust God's perfect plan and pace. We can express gratitude in times of celebration and in times of sorrow. Why? Because God does not change. He stays true to His character and His Word. So, like David, we can depend on the Holy Spirit to help us take each sacred stride with a jubilant proclamation of trust even when things don't go our way. The Holy Spirit has preserved the infallible, God-breathed words of Scripture; therefore, we can expect God to be exactly who He says He is and do exactly what He says

He will do in the Bible. So we can trust His faithfulness and praise Him with joyful expectation in all circumstances—now and forever.

Inhale

> Worship the LORD with gladness;
> come before him with joyful songs.
> (Psalm 100:2)

Exhale

Spirit of the one true God, thanks for knowing us completely and equipping us for each sacred stride You've prepared us to take. Help us to be honest with You about our weaknesses and fears as You gently align our hearts and minds with Your unerring, unchanging truth. Let us be bursting with gratitude for all You've done, all You're doing, and all You promise. As we pray and praise You continually, fuel us with a joy that overflows from Your goodness, compassion, faithfulness, and heart-changing love. In Jesus's name, amen.

SACRED STRIDE

Share how God uses the promise of His faithfulness now and in eternity to fill you with joy, especially when life's circumstances are hard or not what you expected.

16

Peace of Mine

STEP INTO GOD'S WORD
Philippians 4:4–9

STAND ON GOD'S TRUTH
*The Holy Spirit provides the personal peace
required in our most personal spaces.*

While preparing for a family member's wedding in 2022, Ashley grieved as she watched her six-year-old daughter trying on flower girl dresses and admiring the gowns in the bridal shop. She would never take Sadie wedding dress shopping. Sadie's dad would never walk her down the aisle. Their daughter would not make it to adulthood.

Sadie spent the first seventy-three days of her life in the neonatal intensive care unit. Her father's side of the family had a history of Sanfilippo syndrome, a type of childhood dementia. As Ashley prayed, she urged doctors to test their daughter. Though the medical team initially rejected her requests, she remained adamant. After doctors diagnosed three-month-old Sadie, Ashley praised God for providing an answer. Sadly, there is no treatment or cure for Sanfilippo . . . yet. However, the early detection allowed Sadie to receive therapy and become a part of clinical trials, which helped slow the progression of the disease. As Ashley prays for a cure, she raises awareness and encourages others to support research efforts for Sadie and the other children affected by Sanfilippo.

Children with any of the four subtypes of Sanfilippo are usually diagnosed between the ages of four and five. By then most patients have become nonverbal. They may learn daily functions like walking, talking, and feeding themselves—but they will forget everything. Worse, as this progressive genetic disease attacks the central nervous system, the children also suffer from seizures, pain, movement disorders, and loss of mobility. With a life expectancy of ten to twenty years, most children die in their early teens. Sadie turned eight years old in 2024.

After Ashley left the bridal shop in 2022, however, she scheduled a special photo shoot. With her curly hair swooped into a half ponytail, Sadie wore her mama's wedding dress. Though not the real bridal occasion Ashley wanted with her daughter, she thanked God for the moment He'd given her.

Gratitude, however, wasn't always Ashley's first response in the fight to save Sadie's life and the lives of other children with Sanfilippo. She appreciated the family members, friends, and even the strangers they'd met in person and online who rallied around her family. But in the quiet, personal moments when no one was around, Ashley's confidence in God's love and grace enabled her to be honest with Him. She yelled. She cried. Then she relied on the Holy Spirit as she moved forward, because she needed to focus on being Sadie's mom.

God's constant presence became Ashley's safe space. She considered venting her feelings to God to be a powerful way of praying. She used to try making deals with God, promising to do anything if only He would heal Sadie. Eventually, though, she grew to understand that a no from God wasn't a bad thing. Leaning on the power of the Holy Spirit, she could trust everything would be okay no matter what happened. Waiting was hard, but being mad at God didn't feel like an option. She had witnessed Him do too much good in their lives.

Sadie's family and friends remain committed to praying for her and doing all they can to help her live life to the fullest. Knowing things will change, Ashley relies on the power of the Holy Spirit and appreciates every moment in the great life God gave her daughter. But how could Ashley say life was great, considering Sadie's diagnosis? Ashley insists that Sanfilippo will *not* be Sadie's legacy. She sees God in Sadie. At only eight years of age, Sadie makes a difference in Ashley's life and the lives of others simply by being who God created her to be. Her life matters. And God has given Ashley the pleasure and privilege of being Sadie's mom.

So Ashley rejoices in the relentless peace of the Spirit's constant presence, grateful for every extraordinary moment in Sadie's life. Though Sadie won't remember those moments, Ashley will. And whether Sadie is cured physically here or by going home with Jesus, either way, Ashley declares that "Sanfilippo will not win. God wins!"

In Philippians 4:4 the apostle Paul called the church to a seemingly impossible charge: "Rejoice in the Lord always. I will say it again: Rejoice!" He invited believers to step into an ongoing state of joy dependent on God's constant presence in the moment, not on fleeting feelings or ever-changing circumstances. This joy overflows from the peace of abiding in Him, cleaving to Him, simply being with Him. The Spirit of God enables us to let our "gentleness be evident to all" *because* "the Lord is near" (v. 5).

After we've accepted Christ as our personal Savior and submitted to Him as Lord, nothing we say, do, think, feel, or forget can affect the Spirit's indwelling. Scripture affirms that we cannot lose our salvation or change anything about the Holy Spirit. But how do we walk by faith when every fiber of our being says we cannot endure our seemingly hopeless situations? Should we believe God never gives us anything we can't handle? No—that's a misinterpretation of Scripture.* God can and does give us more than we can handle so we can know our depravity and our desperate need for Him. And He makes Himself available always.

Paul said, "Do not be anxious about anything, but in every situation, by prayer and petition, with thanksgiving, present your requests to God" (v. 6). The apostle's words affirm that believers will feel uneasy, nervous, worried, restless, and even fearful at times. However, we don't have to remain anxious, because anxiety does not define (nor does it defile) our core identity as Christ followers. No feelings we experience have that power.

We can approach God with an expectant faith built on our certainty of who He is and what He has said. We can pray and praise Him with a deep sense of gratitude for all He has done, is doing, and has promised to do. When we pray, our hearts and minds will be guarded by "the peace of God, which transcends all understanding," not in the security of our circumstances but "in Christ Jesus" (v. 7). We can't find the peace we need in the temporary solutions or even through the support or comfort of others during our suffering. The peace we need comes from God Himself, peace we can experience even when we're still in the trenches of affliction.

* First Corinthians 10:13 is commonly misunderstood to mean we'll never be overwhelmed by circumstances. But that's not what the verse says and not what it means.

Paul demonstrated how tightly woven our thinking patterns are to our sense of peace. He said, "Finally, brothers and sisters, whatever is true, whatever is noble, whatever is right, whatever is pure, whatever is lovely, whatever is admirable—if anything is excellent or praiseworthy—think about such things" (v. 8). When God takes up space in our minds, when we're actively seeking and acknowledging Him, He enables us to submit to Him so that we can surrender every thought to Him. Through this ongoing act of worship, He renews or changes our thinking and aligns our heart with His Word.

Moment-by-moment dependence on the Holy Spirit teaches us to recognize His fingerprints in the extraordinary-ordinary moments of life. "And the God of peace will be with [us]" (v. 9). The "God of peace," not just the peace of God. We're not promised an adequate portion of God's peace, just enough to get through the afflictions we encounter during our lowest valley moments. Rather, God Himself—the establisher of peace, harmony, and well-being—remains with us constantly. We can rejoice because the Holy Spirit, who dwells in us always, provides the very personal peace required in our most personal spaces. The Holy Spirit *is* our peace everlasting.

Inhale

> Whatever you have learned or received or heard from me, or seen in me—put it into practice. And the God of peace will be with you. (Philippians 4:9)

Exhale

Spirit of God, thanks for promising to be our peace when everything around us seems to be falling apart and when worries are biting at our heels. Be our peace when what we fear most feels like tumultuous waves smashing us against the jagged rocks of a lonely shore. Be our peace as we hunker down in the trenches of Your unchanging truth. Thank You for every moment You've proven Yourself to be faithful, good, loving, and in control. Help us trust that You are always our peace *with us*. In Jesus's name, amen.

SACRED STRIDE

Thank the Holy Spirit for His peace-giving refuge, sovereign goodness, and sufficient grace in the quiet spaces of your life, when no one else is around. Ask Him to empower and comfort you with the peace of His constant presence as you walk by faith through every situation, especially those that feel too big or too hard to endure.

17

Unfailing Fortitude

STEP INTO GOD'S WORD
Psalm 40

STAND ON GOD'S TRUTH
The Holy Spirit's unending presence provides our
unfailing fortitude, no matter how we feel.

Raised by faith-filled parents, Manuel and Ernestine, Katara grew up feeling loved. She believed that all she needed to be successful was Jesus, education, and prayer. Fueled by the desire to excel, she began checking off her goals at the age of eighteen. But she also began turning away from some of her family values when she went to college, ignoring God and diving into the party scene. Others saw the picture of success Katara wanted them to see. But relationships and party after party failed to fill her emptiness. Then one day she asked God to fix *everything*.

The next day, Katara accepted a party invitation from a friend. She never expected she'd be attending a Christian fellowship. She definitely did not expect to answer an altar call and recommit her life to Jesus. But that's what happened—and Katara spent the next fifteen years on fire for God.

During that fired-up faith season, Katara landed her dream job and felt close to God. So her persisting feelings of emptiness confused her. She shrugged off her emotions, understanding that she couldn't always be on a high in her walk with God. However, at the age of thirty-five, she admitted that her career, her relationships, and her life were not going as she had planned. Though Katara recognized that part of her diagnosed depression was chemical, she knew her deferred dreams contributed to the way she felt.

A close friend prayed with Katara and encouraged her to try a therapist, someone close to her workplace who wouldn't minimize or diminish her faith. She began making strides in therapy—until her mother suffered a heart attack. Katara returned home immediately, grateful God gave her the opportunity to say goodbye to her mom before she passed.

As Katara helped plan the funeral, though, she shut down her grief. She spent the next few years going from home to work, then back to her sofa each day. Despite great relationships with her dad, other family members, and friends, Katara felt alone. She prayed constantly, but nothing seemed to change.

One day the Holy Spirit nudged her to attend the later service at church so she could go to a friend's baby shower. And for the first time in a long time, she felt good. God used that incident to remind Katara of the importance of community, and from then on she reengaged.

Also, after allowing herself a mourning period guided by her therapist, Katara prayerfully stepped back into the dating scene. She married a God-fearing man after her thirty-seventh birthday. Two years later, God blessed them with a baby girl. Katara praised God for equipping her with tools to manage her depression and anxiety so she could be the wife and mother He created her to be. Knowing that the Holy Spirit had brought her out of depression before helped her trust He would bring her through again if those feelings resurfaced.

Though she still sometimes struggled even during the good times, the Holy Spirit helped her work through her low feelings and dark thoughts. And through Katara's healing journey, God cultivated in her a desire to raise awareness and help erase the stigma that surrounds mental illnesses within faith communities. She began writing to encourage others to step out of their silent suffering. She even wrote a book in which she emphasized the need for prayer, patience, and practical tools.

Katara understood that some days she just wasn't going to feel her best. No one jumps from mountaintop to mountaintop; everyone has to travel through the valleys with God too. As the Spirit of God lovingly affirmed to Katara that her feelings were valid, He reminded her that those feelings were not the foundation of her faith. Depression, like all suffering, consists of passing moments. And God promised He would always be with her and bring her through *everything*. The Spirit's unending presence provided Katara's unfailing fortitude, the strength of mind she needed to live with courageous faith moment by moment.

Throughout Scripture, we can witness God's people trusting Him while facing worry, anxiety, fear, and even depression. The psalmist David testified: "I waited patiently for the LORD; he turned to me and heard my cry. He lifted me out of the slimy pit, out of the mud and mire; he set my feet on a rock and gave me a firm place to stand" (Psalm 40:1–2). That firm place is God's presence. The type of slimy pit or mud and mire we wallow in doesn't make any difference to our compassionate God. He knows His beloved children can suffer from real mental illnesses like depression and anxiety simply because they are realities of living in a fallen world.

Our hope-giving God gives us a "new song" testifying to His greatness (v. 3). Blessings come to "the one who trusts in the Lord" (v. 4), not the one who has it all together all the time, who never slips up, backslides, or feels stuck. God weaves His grace through every twist, turn, and time-out we experience during our messiest moments.

Through the power of the Holy Spirit, we can praise Him and pray with boldness *while* we're weeping in pits and trudging down muddy trails in the valley. We can rejoice because all circumstances, even our most challenging hardships, are passing events, fleeting moments, blips on the radar of the great plans God has for each of us. So we can join the psalmist and sing, "Many, Lord my God, are the wonders you have done, the things you planned for us. None can compare with you; were I to speak and tell of your deeds, they would be too many to declare" (v. 5). Hallelujah!

David discovered the freedom to falter and even fail. He said, "I desire to do your will, my God; your law is within my heart" (v. 8). Yet having that genuine desire to do God's will and having God's law tucked in his heart did not mean David was perfect or that his journey would be without struggle. He proclaimed, "I do not hide your righteousness in my heart; I speak of your faithfulness and your saving help. I do not conceal your love and your faithfulness from the great assembly" (v. 10). David unashamedly shared what God had done for him and how God used the ugly messes of his life to create a beautiful mosaic of grace.

David fervently asked God to "be pleased" to save him and "come quickly" to help him (v. 13), then continued: "May all who seek you rejoice and be glad in you; may those who long for your saving help always say, 'The LORD is great!'" (v. 16). Admitting his neediness, David asked God to think of him. "You are my help and my deliverer," he said. "You are my God, do not delay" (v. 17). David trusted that God loved him enough to keep track of him.

The Holy Spirit knows the deepest desires of our hearts and our greatest struggles, even those we're keeping secret or have yet to recognize. Whether we're dealing with an illness or the consequences of our sin, He will not lose sight of us or let go of us. As we rely on the Holy Spirit moment by moment, even in the darkest trenches, we can navigate our complex emotions with the help of the personal community *and* the medical community He has established for us. No feeling or diagnosis can destroy us or separate us from the God who loves us. The Holy Spirit's unending presence will always be our unfailing fortitude as we take one sacred stride of faith at a time.

Inhale

> I waited patiently for the LORD;
>> he turned to me and heard my cry.
> He lifted me out of the slimy pit,
>> out of the mud and mire;
> he set my feet on a rock
>> and gave me a firm place to stand.
> (Psalm 40:1–2)

Exhale

Compassionate Spirit, thanks for remaining gentle with us and helping us to be gentle with ourselves and others. When our ever-changing feelings seem like determining factors in our lives, remind us that You never change and never leave us to fend for ourselves. Help us reach out to You and others when we're struggling with depression, anxiety, worry, low feelings, or dark thoughts. Help us determine if we need professional help too. Increase our patience with You and ourselves as we trust Your unending presence to provide our unfailing fortitude today and every day, no matter how we feel. In Jesus's name, amen.

SACRED STRIDE

Ask the Holy Spirit to reveal if you or someone you love is suffering from bouts of depression, anxiety, or worry. If that someone is you, ask Him to help you get support immediately. And ask Him to be your strength as you support others who are battling mental illnesses or struggling through triggered bouts of depression or anxiety.

18

A Lifestyle of Service

STEP INTO GOD'S WORD
1 Peter 4:1–11

STAND ON GOD'S TRUTH
The Holy Spirit equips us with unique gifts and opportunities to love and serve others.

Jake wanted to serve God with his life, just like his grandparents. He also wanted to work with dogs, so he studied clinical psychology and animal and canine psychology. He graduated from Animal Behavior College, received credentials from the Certification Council of Professional Dog Trainers in 2011, and committed to taking thirty-six credits every three years to maintain his credentials. When Jake met his wife, Amanda, they started training their dogs to serve as therapy dogs and visiting a local live-in care facility for senior citizens.

Then one day a household-name movie celebrity, who was a friend of a family in need, donated the funds for Jake to purchase and train a service dog for an injured girl. After seeing how God used their dog, Jake and Amanda started praying specifically. They began looking for their own facility to train service dogs. God provided support through people Jake knew and others who knew about Jake's integrity, kindness, and dedication to serving others generously and sacrificially. Jake's grandparents believed he was doing God's work. They prayed for him and encouraged him to follow his dreams. When his grandfather passed in 2013, Jake's grandmother surprised him with the seed money that helped secure a loan to start the ministry of Tails for Life. In February 2014, Jake and Amanda opened a day school in a rental space and committed to training one service dog at a time. As word got out, however, the community rallied around them. Tails for Life opened the doors of their own facility in July of 2016. And Jake credited God with every step of the process.

In early 2017, the state of Wisconsin added Tails for Life as an eligible resource for the Children's Long-Term Support Program, which accepts service dogs as medical equipment. Tails for Life began accepting waivers for service dog training. The county case workers would contact Jake regarding a child to determine if he or she would benefit from a service dog. The county did all the paperwork, usually within thirty days, and reserved the training spot with funds. Then the state paid the remaining fees and reimbursed the county.

Tails for Life worked with any county in Wisconsin and trained four service dogs in the spring and four in the fall. Not all dogs graduated from the program, though. Some dogs couldn't properly do the tasks. Some had medical or behavioral issues. Some weren't motivated to work. So Jake planned on dropping one or two dogs from the program every year. But he never let the families or the county pay extra costs if a dog failed. The Tails for Life team worked hard on fundraisers to keep the training costs lower and to cover the losses if a dog didn't graduate. They also interviewed families to ensure the well-trained pets went to good homes. Jake declared that every dog, even those with a rough start, had a chance to be great with a purpose and with God. He believed the same about people.

Serving in such a unique ministry often came with unexpected challenges, though. Some clients gave Jake a tough time. Sometimes finances were tight. But whenever he felt like quitting, Jake prayed—a lot, especially for others. He depended on the Holy Spirit to help him persevere. And every time Jake asked God for help, God did something to encourage him.

Working around the clock, Jake considered training dogs to be a lifestyle with no days off—just as doing God's work is a round-the-clock lifestyle for a Christian. Jake thanked God for his partners in ministry, especially Amanda; their daughter, Kinslee; and his praying grandma. They believed God was using every dog trained through Tails for Life. Relying on the Holy Spirit one sacred stride at a time, Jake continued to believe that loving people and training dogs were his God-given purpose, his lifestyle, and God's work.

The apostle Peter draws believers in Jesus to focus on His promised return as they embrace a lifestyle dedicated to God's purpose while remaining dependent on God's power (1 Peter 4:1–6). Peter encourages believers in God the Son to live with an eternal perspective so that they may effectively pray (v. 7). When God's people pray, God answers and guides their way. More importantly, we're made to serve God by serving others in love. Peter said, "Above all, love each other deeply, because love covers over a multitude of sins. Offer hospitality to one another without grumbling" (vv. 8–9). Expressing God's love and hospitality, which is simply generosity and kindness, is an act of service that looks different for each one of us.

Any way we serve others is an expression of worship and our love for God. Peter wrote, "Each of you should use whatever gift you have received to serve others, as faithful stewards of God's grace in its various forms" (v. 10). Though God listed only a few gifts in Scripture, Peter's use of "whatever gift" reminds us that all gifts, talents, skills, and abilities can be used to serve God and His people. When we're living to please God, we can dedicate all we have as a love-offering to honor Him—the Giver of all good things. Even our passions and past experiences prepare us to do God's work when we're committed to a lifestyle of service. Peter said, "If anyone speaks, they should do so as one who speaks the very words of God. If anyone serves, they should do so with the strength God provides, so that in all things God may be praised through Jesus Christ. To him be the glory and the power for ever and ever. Amen" (v. 11).

All types of service and all the unique ways we express love for others "with the strength God provides" bring God glory and praise. We're designed to use our gifts according to His plan and for the benefit of all the people He created and loves, not just those who look like us or believe as we do. God can use anyone and anything, at any time, in any way—just like He's using Jake, a dog trainer who has committed to a lifestyle of loving and serving Jesus and people every day in his own unique way.

Inhale

Each of you should use whatever gift you have received to serve others, as faithful stewards of God's grace in its various forms. (1 Peter 4:10)

Exhale

Generous Spirit of God, thanks for the limitlessly creative ways You've designed us to serve You and others. Reveal how You want us to love others in kind, practical, and unique ways. Please provide the tools, the opportunities, and the power for us to honor You with a lifestyle of generous love and faithful service. Show us the next sacred stride You want us to take and surround us with supportive people. Bring to mind ways we can support others who are using their gifts in creative ways for Your glory. In Jesus's name, amen.

SACRED STRIDE

Ask the Holy Spirit to help you create a list of practical ways you can use your God-given dreams, talents, skills, abilities, and experiences to serve others through selfless acts of kindness. Then prayerfully start pursuing your dreams by embracing a lifestyle of service to God.

19

Fueled by God's Goodness

STEP INTO GOD'S WORD
Psalm 37

STAND ON GOD'S TRUTH
The Holy Spirit helps us serve generously and
graciously from the bounty of His goodness.

In 1986, Jana was only forty-two when her sixty-four-year-old father got cancer. She had no idea that she was beginning a lifetime of serving as a caregiver, while working full-time as a school administrator and singing in the choir with her husband of twenty-three years, Bob. Three years later, before her father died, he told her to take "good care" of her mother too. Jana and Bob bought the house next door to her mother's. They never had children, but family was important to them. They wanted her sixty-five-year-old mom to remain in her home. Soon after, though, Jana had a car accident and started having neck issues that required surgery. She wore a brace and did physical therapy for six weeks, which relieved her pain enough

121

to begin preparing for her new home. However, nine months before their move in 1996, Bob had his first brain surgery—a craniotomy.

In her late forties, Jana began caring for her mother *and* her husband. Bob had to relearn how to walk, talk, eat, and more. The following year, he had his second craniotomy. Four years later, in 2001, Bob's third craniotomy forced him to stop working. Jana became the main provider for their family. After Bob's fourth brain surgery in 2003, Jana worked full-time during the day while caring for her husband and her mother full-time at night.

As an evaluator for teachers earning their credentials, some days she would drive almost one hundred miles round trip to visit classrooms. While driving alone, she worshiped God by praying and singing hymns. After working a full day, Jana cooked, cleaned, and cared for her husband and mother until 9:00 p.m., sometimes later. She also worked two and sometimes three extra jobs in retail and with the school district. Jana never complained, even when she began experiencing severe neck pain again in 2020.

When overwhelmed by her responsibilities, Jana trusted God would care for her because Scripture says He would. She said "I know" prayers to keep her anchored in the Word of God: "I know You are my strength, Holy Spirit. I know You are faithful and in control, Father. I know You love me, Jesus." Relying on the Spirit to help her live out Matthew 5:16, Jana often quoted Jesus's words: "In the same way, let your light shine before others, that they may see your good deeds and glorify your Father in heaven."

In 2022, Jana's mother died. Jana couldn't face the empty seat beside her at church. As she grieved and prayed, God led Jana and Bob to a new church. After their second visit, they joined the choir. The songs, rich in biblical truth, became one of the ways God deepened Jana's faith and strengthened her resolve. But in September 2023, doctors diagnosed Jana with Sjögren's, an autoimmune disease that made her life even more challenging. In 2024, on her seventy-sixth birthday, she was also diagnosed with pemphigus. Her second autoimmune disease caused severe food allergies, weight and hair loss, and painful skin abrasions. Still, Jana continued working and serving as a caregiver full-time while singing in the choir with Bob.

In August 2024, Jana and Bob celebrated their fiftieth anniversary. Seventy-six-year-old Jana finally retired from her career in public education in December of that same year. Though Jana's health declined, the Holy Spirit empowered her to keep her relationship with God a priority. She continued to read Scripture and worship through song with Bob, who is a mighty prayer warrior and still remembers Scriptures he learned as a child.

Fueled by God's goodness and love, Jana serves others while exuding joy and peace. She greets others with a genuine smile and a warm hug, encourages others, and gives generously, even when she doesn't have much to give. Jana understands she can lose everything and everyone, but she can never lose God. She trusts His promises as she relies on the Holy Spirit to provide all she needs to lovingly serve and share with others freely. No matter how hard her circumstances, Jana perseveres in faith and trusts God is good, always, because she believes that every God-breathed word of Scripture is true.

In the Old Testament, God the Father used the messianic promise of God the Son and the anointing of God the Spirit to give the psalmist David enduring faith. David's life was far from perfect; he did, however, devote himself to placing God first, even when times were hard. David encouraged others to keep their eyes on the eternal and unchanging God, especially during difficult or unjust circumstances. He sang, "Do not fret because of those who are evil or be envious of those who do wrong; for like the grass they will soon wither, like green plants they will soon die away" (Psalm 37:1–2). David knew evil couldn't win and sin would never be worth envying or fretting over, regardless of the world's awful injustices or his own very real struggles and limitations.

The psalmist offers steadfast hope for those who want to live God-centered lives. He wrote, "Trust in the LORD and do good; dwell in the land and enjoy safe pasture. Take delight in the LORD, and he will give you the desires of your heart" (vv. 3–4). David notes that there is a condition to God giving us the desires of our hearts. We must first "take delight" in Him, which means to be fulfilled by God alone, to enjoy His presence, and to place Him above all things, especially the desires of our flesh. When we do this, our desires change so that we want what God wants.

When we believe what God says in His Word and put Him first, we can enter a safe space that enables us to trust Him. Embracing His desires as our own, we can do good because of His faithful goodness. His persistent presence makes a life of joy and peace possible.

Through the anointing of the Spirit, David encouraged God-first living and wrote many of the "I know" prayers recorded in Psalms. In a world that dishonored, minimized, and rejected God, the Spirit empowered David to commit his way to the Lord (v. 5). David trusted God to handle the judging. And God would see to it that the rewards would outshine any problems or injustice David might face (v. 6). Like David, we can "be still before the LORD and wait patiently for him" to work (v. 7). We don't have to expend our energy trying to do

124

God's job, because the outcome of the battle is certain; "Those who are evil will be destroyed" (vv. 8–9).

God knows that living for Him on this side of eternity will not be easy. So the Holy Spirit provides the security of His presence and the surety of His promises. We can rest in the assurance of our eternal inheritance guaranteed by our hope in the Lord. No matter how difficult our day-to-day journey becomes, He refreshes us so we can serve others generously and graciously.

We don't always have to smile or *feel* joyful to exude joy and peace. Amid our struggles, our lives can still be marked by compassion, faithfulness, and integrity. The Spirit's anointing and steadfast love for us make our kindness feel genuine to others. He can make joy infectious and draw people to Himself through us. And when we grow weary from suffering, the Holy Spirit drives our perseverance. We can sing His praises and, through "I know" prayers, proclaim His name as we depend on His grace and goodness to fuel our faith.

Inhale

> Trust in the LORD and do good;
>> dwell in the land and enjoy safe pasture.
> (Psalm 37:3)

Exhale

Replenishing Spirit, thanks for giving us what we need, even when our needs differ from our wants or what we think is best. Make us known for our goodness toward others as we love from the overflow of Your abundant goodness toward us. When we're hurting or weary, breathe peace and hope into us. Give us courage to set wise, healthy boundaries and rest in You.

As we trust You to carry our burdens, please help us speak "I know" prayers with faith fueled by Your promises and Your joy-giving presence. In Jesus's name, amen.

SACRED STRIDE

Ask the Spirit to help you create a list of "I know" prayers based on Bible verses.

20

Forever Faithful

STEP INTO GOD'S WORD
2 Thessalonians 2:13–3:5

STAND ON GOD'S TRUTH
*The Holy Spirit empowers our victory through
every "Yes, Lord!" and "Help, Lord!" we pray.*

Arthur was born in 1948 and raised in Kansas City, Kansas. He recalled a brand of social consciousness and labeling that was so inbred and so much a part of life that he knew his place and role in society as an African American. He followed the societal narrative of what he could and could not do. Back-door entries at restaurants, separate and unequal schooling . . . such things were his reality.

At the age of fifteen Arthur accepted Jesus as his Savior and Lord. He believed in his immediate freedom in Christ. He embraced the Holy Spirit's work in freeing him from the penalty of sin and transforming him to be more like Jesus over time. He placed his hope in the promise of eternity in heaven. The trajectory of his life changed inwardly.

But the external things didn't change. He was still an African American in this world.

The Holy Spirit used Arthur's varied experiences, good and bad, to stretch his faith and deepen his understanding of Scripture and ministry. When he went to college, his social and educational world expanded. He listened to good Bible teaching on Christian radio and eventually went to seminary for graduate school. As the Spirit nurtured his heart in seeking holiness, Arthur's world continued broadening, as did his love for God, His Word, and His people.

In 1988, Arthur served as an associate pastor on Chicago's West Side with a multiethnic but predominately African American congregation. During that time, he also worked for a Christian publisher and became an editor for multiethnic Sunday school literature. Arthur remembered having to "step up his game" by learning more about African American history. As he lived and served on the West Side of Chicago, he experienced a greater degree of social awareness and engagement. The Spirit used his boots-on-the-ground experience to develop in him more mercy and a deeper understanding of racial and social injustice.

In 1994, Arthur accepted his second pastoral role at Judson Baptist Church. He was the first African American pastor to lead a then predominately White congregation on the dividing line of Chicago and Oak Park. His church was featured in *The Elusive Dream: The Power of Race in Interracial Churches* by Korie Little Edwards, originally published in 2008. Arthur shared the vision statement that the church created at Judson: "Standing courageously at the intersection where race and class collide and daring to live out authentic Christian community."

From 2006 to the fall of 2016, Arthur served in his third pastoral post as an associate pastor at another church. The leadership wanted a multiethnic church like he had at Judson. They understood that in order to reach the city, they needed a pastoral team that looked like the city.

Finally, retiring after nearly three decades of leading in pastoral roles in the Chicago area, Arthur moved back to Kansas and served in a behind-the-scenes ministry. He offered coaching, crisis support, and consulting to pastors and other leaders.

As Arthur reflected on his journey, he realized that when God captures a person's heart in ways that transcend the things that may have molded him or her, that person could no longer be bound by those things. Though each person needed to be in touch with their past, no one needs to be limited by it.

In 2024, Arthur celebrated seventy-six (and counting) years on this earth. He has remained forever faithful to "Yes, Lord! living." He declared that "Yes, Lord!" and "Help, Lord!" are the greatest words he could ever utter. He said, "God is equipping His servants for the work that still needs to be done. We need an outpour of His Spirit so that no one will ask, 'Did God do that?' We need such an outpour so that no one will need to ask if God is among us. We need an outpour of God's Spirit that changes us personally *and* changes the landscape of the church. And when we're awakened to the greatness of our God, we can fulfill our roles in this world in the name of Jesus."

Arthur's anticipation for the strengthening and expansion of the church rings with the apostle Paul's similar, faith-filled joy in his letter to the diverse Thessalonian church. Hearing of their steadfastness under great persecution, Paul longed to encourage them for the road ahead. The apostle expressed thankfulness because his "brothers and sisters loved by the Lord" were chosen "to be saved through the sanctifying work of the Spirit and through belief in the truth" (2 Thessalonians

2:13). Paul acknowledged his part in their faith journey but maintained that Jesus was the one who called the believers to faith (v. 14).

Paul urged the Thessalonian church to continue in faithfulness, to "stand firm" against false teaching and persecution and "hold fast" to the sound doctrine they had been taught, "whether by word of mouth or by letter" (v. 15). Emphasizing their dependence on God, Paul prayed, "May our Lord Jesus Christ himself and God our Father, who loved us and by his grace gave us eternal encouragement and good hope, encourage your hearts and strengthen you in every good deed and word" (vv. 16–17). His words reveal his trust in God's reliability and His ability to strengthen and expand the church: "Pray for us that the message of the Lord may spread rapidly and be honored, just as it was with you" (2 Thessalonians 3:1).

Like Arthur, we can trust the Holy Spirit will empower us to utter, "Yes, Lord!" and "Help, Lord!" with every sacred stride God leads us to take. When we make ourselves available to God, we can experience an outpour of His Spirit. As we seek Him and surrender to Him, He can transform us and the beautifully diverse church He is building in such a way that others recognize our forever-faithful God is indeed among us. Hallelujah!

Inhale

> May our Lord Jesus Christ himself and God our Father, who loved us and by his grace gave us eternal encouragement and good hope, encourage your hearts and strengthen you in every good deed and word. (2 Thessalonians 2:16–17)

Exhale

Faithful Spirit of God, please forgive the wickedness of our past as individuals and as a community of Your beautifully diverse image-bearers. Thanks for intentionally creating diversity in Your kingdom and unifying us through Christ as You empower us to serve You together. Help us acknowledge Your constant, life-transforming presence. Make us well-known for our "Yes, Lord!" and "Help, Lord!" living. And help us see and love every neighbor You've created, every neighbor You love and use for Your glory. We need an outpour of Your Spirit so we'll look like Jesus, live like Jesus, and love like Jesus. In Jesus's name, amen.

SACRED STRIDE

List the evidence of the Holy Spirit's faithfulness in every aspect of your life. Then ask Him to show you practical ways to serve, courageously and compassionately, within His diverse church, one "Yes, Lord!" and "Help, Lord!" at a time.

21

God's Gentle Hands

STEP INTO GOD'S WORD
Psalm 116

STAND ON GOD'S TRUTH
*The Holy Spirit's gentleness with us stirs
graciousness in our hearts toward others.*

Kari grew up in a Christian home, got married at the age of eighteen, had her first daughter, and got divorced at nineteen. A few years later, as a single mom in her early twenties and attending college, Kari got married and had her second child, a son. The young family flourished for two years before Kari became a grieving widow and the single mom of two children. She didn't have the time or desire to date, but James persisted in courting her. She married him a year later.

Though James loved both of Kari's children as his own, they wanted to have a baby together. They prayed as they struggled with infertility. Since both had worked with children who had disabilities, they decided to adopt a child with Down syndrome. The adoption fell through.

Three years later, Kari found out she was pregnant—a

miracle! Two years after the birth of her third child, Kari got pregnant again. Another miracle. At twenty-one weeks, however, the doctors discovered that the child, Leila, had multiple anomalies. Knowing God had a purpose for Leila, the couple began fighting for the life of their unborn child. And everything seemed to be going fine—until doctors informed them that Leila had trisomy 18, a serious genetic disorder.

Doctors tried to convince the couple that an "early induction," a termination of pregnancy, would be best. They pressured James by saying Kari could die. Although they later discovered this was a scare tactic, James and Kari believed the risk was real. They, however, wanted God to decide if Leila lived. Realizing the doctors had given up on their daughter, they asked the Holy Spirit to strengthen them and lead them to a medical team who would fight for Leila's life.

In the meantime, James legally adopted Kari's son, since his biological dad was dead. They wanted to make sure he could stay with James if Kari didn't come home from the hospital. They also planned Leila's funeral and picked out her burial plot. As the couple continued praying, they remained steadfast in their decision to let God decide what was best for their whole family.

Thirty-four weeks into Kari's pregnancy, the Holy Spirit filled the couple with hope for their baby girl. They transferred to a different hospital and began seeing specialists. Sadly, however, their new medical team agreed that Leila would die immediately after birth. The cardiologist said they needed to deliver immediately if they wanted any chance of seeing Leila alive. The couple cried out to God. If their daughter was going to die, they wanted to know that they had done all they could.

Leila lived!

In December 2024, family and friends celebrated Leila's

thirteen years of life. God continued growing their family through adoption and fostering children with disabilities. Whenever the couple felt weary or weak, the Holy Spirit recharged their faith. He provided support for each of them and helped them support each other. He surrounded them with a caring community and used them to encourage others.

Kari often suffered from a form of survivor's guilt when other families lost their children to trisomy 18. Still, she thanked God for His gentleness over the years. She continued advocating for awareness and research as she offered families compassionate prayers, encouragement, and practical support. The songs Kari chose for Leila's funeral became the songs the Holy Spirit used to help her keep fighting for their family and praising God for Leila's life thirteen years and counting.

With a similar tone of gratitude, the writer of Psalm 116 wrote, "I love the LORD, for he heard my voice; he heard my cry for mercy. Because he turned his ear to me, I will call on him as long as I live" (vv. 1–2).

The psalmist's love for the Lord flowed from a heart intimately familiar with God's faithfulness, goodness, dependability, and gentleness within a covenant relationship. "Entangled" by the "cords of death," the psalmist confessed the depth of his "distress and sorrow" (v. 3). While his own imminent physical death was his personal concern, his imagery easily expresses our own fear of losing a loved one, or of some other great loss, even the death of a dream.

The psalmist responded to his inner turmoil with confidence that God was always listening, caring, and ready to intercede. He wrote, "Then I called on the name of the LORD: 'LORD, save me!'" (v. 4). These are words from a heart that understands no grief is too small or too big to place in God's loving hands. The psalmist's personal testimony is a public love offering to the one true God: "The Lord is gracious and righteous; our God is full of compassion. The Lord protects the unwary; when I was brought low, he saved me" (vv. 5–6). Hallelujah! Here is a powerful promise of hope and comfort to all God's children facing affliction. "Return to your rest, my soul," the writer says, "for the Lord has been good to you" (v. 7). Though death was a real possibility, the Lord *is* a deliverer, and the psalmist trusted His power to keep him walking "in the land of the living" (vv. 8–9). In the face of his troubles and shortcomings, he poured out a praise-filled prayer of gratitude: "What shall I return to the Lord for all his goodness to me?" (vv. 10–12). His answer: a life of loyalty. He would live for the Lord obediently, proclaiming His name publicly (vv. 13–14). For he knew God's love. He recognized how preciously God values "his faithful servants"—each and every one, including the psalmist himself (v. 15).

Celebrating his legacy of faith, the psalm writer promised to be grateful and generous as he worshiped the Lord (vv. 16–17). He would "fulfill [his] vows to the Lord in the presence of all his people, in the courts of the house of the Lord" . . . ultimately and inevitably in God's constant presence (vv. 18–19).

With a final cry of praise, the psalmist devoted himself to being a living testimony, ready to surrender to God, submit to God, serve God, and share God with others.

As for Leila?

The Holy Spirit's presence, with His almighty and always gentle hand of compassion, is still evident in each wonderful moment of her beautiful life. His love and joy radiate through her contagious smile and bright eyes. Her mere existence is proof that God loves His image-bearers, hears our prayers, and continues to be an all-powerful miracle worker today, just as

He was in the Old and New Testament times. As we celebrate Leila's life and the Spirit's anointing over James and Kari in their love and care for the children God has entrusted to them, we can trust God to be gentle with us too.

Inhale

> The LORD is gracious and righteous;
> our God is full of compassion.
> (Psalm 116:5)

Exhale

Gentle Spirit, thanks for being so tender and patient with us. Thanks for extending Your sufficient grace when we need it most. Thanks for reminding us that we're worth loving simply because You created us, not because of what we are or are not able to do. Help us receive Your healing mercy as You make us more compassionate toward others who need mercy. As we inhale the hope of Your unfailing Word and exhale words of faith secured by the peace of Your constant presence, give us courage to stand up for those who cannot advocate for themselves. In Jesus's name, amen.

SACRED STRIDE

Ask the Holy Spirit to help you create a list that includes the ways He has been and is gentle with you. Then ask Him to show you how you can show tenderness to a beloved image-bearer, affirming that person's value just because he or she is created by God.

22

Who's in Control?

STEP INTO GOD'S WORD
2 Peter 1:1–11

STAND ON GOD'S TRUTH
*The Holy Spirit fuels our self-control so we can
honor Him with our God-given freedom.*

Geoffrey stole his first pack of cigarettes in seventh grade. He started smoking marijuana while priding himself in playing the roles of star student, athlete, and pastor's kid. When his weekend drug use no longer satisfied him, he tried opioids. He used drugs while going to class and church—until the district suspended him during his junior year of high school.

The suspension didn't feel like a painful consequence, though. While other kids were getting the book thrown at them, he got lawyers, treatment centers, and extra chances. Recognizing and utilizing his privilege, eighteen-year-old Geoffrey graduated early and went to college—where he discovered a drug that was cheaper, easier to obtain, and harder to quit.

Heroin.

Geoffrey could no longer function *without* drugs. He began

stealing and failing classes. When he got caught carrying a gun, his parents refused to bail him out and insisted he seek professional help. After getting kicked out of his first residential treatment center, twenty-year-old Geoffrey entered another center far away from everyone he knew. He tried being a part-time user, but drugs were stronger and easier to buy in Nashville. He went to jail, mental hospitals, and rehab. The toxic cycle continued until Geoffrey, only twenty-one, overdosed while driving and crashed into a telephone pole. Finally he called his parents for help and checked into a Christian rehab facility.

As Geoffrey struggled with his addictions, he avoided the chapel on campus. He had been baptized before he started using drugs, but he wasn't happy with God. He thought God had created him wrong. While Geoffrey wrestled with his faith, the Holy Spirit reminded him of a Bible verse he didn't remember memorizing: "When you pass through the waters, I will be with you; and when you pass through the rivers, they will not sweep over you. When you walk through the fire, you will not be burned; the flames will not set you ablaze" (Isaiah 43:2). Still, the temptation to use drugs grew stronger.

One night Geoffrey tried to find a dealer and failed, which was a miracle. He returned to the center and met Daniel, a Christian man who welcomed his questions and offered to explore the Bible with him in search of answers. Nine months later—after months of studying the Bible and praying with Daniel—Geoffrey realized he was sober *and* happy. He hadn't even thought about drugs.

Geoffrey recalled how past programs reinforced the "once an addict, always an addict" belief system. He tied his identity to addiction instead of Christ when he said, "Hello, I'm Geoffrey. I'm an addict." As the Holy Spirit helped him accept his freedom in Christ, Geoffrey realized that he was not an addict or a criminal for life. He was a new creation, a much-loved child of God!

Focused on nurturing authentic relationships with God and others, Geoffrey came alongside his father to write a book to encourage others who were affected by drug abuse or praying for prodigals. And after Geoffrey married Sarah, they began serving the Lord together. He prayed for the cultivation of self-control in his life as the Spirit empowered him to relinquish every desire for control. He surrendered to and depended on the Spirit one moment at a time. God uncovered the reasons Geoffrey wanted to numb himself, rebuked the thought patterns that had led to relapse in the past, and enabled him to watch for triggers. Instead of trying to white-knuckle through temptation, Geoffrey opened his palms and reached for Jesus.

The apostle Peter encouraged believers that "[God's] divine power has given us everything we need for a godly life through our knowledge of him who called us by his own glory and goodness" (2 Peter 1:3). Through Jesus we've *received* His promises, which free us from bondage to sin (v. 4). "Received" is an action in the past tense, which means believers have accepted the promises God gave. Our intimate relationship with Jesus allows us to "make every effort to add" different qualities to our faith (v. 5). We can grow in goodness, knowledge, self-control, perseverance, godliness, mutual affection, and love, so that we can more faithfully reflect God the Son's character (vv. 5–8). These characteristics are the fruit of the Spirit in Galatians 5:22–23, produced by the Holy Spirit's power, not human efforts. The fruit of the Spirit flourishes in unity as a whole and in harmony with our surrender to Him.

When believers "possess these qualities in increasing measure"—which implies a commitment to nurturing our spiritual growth—we can avoid being "ineffective and unproductive" as we live in relationship with Jesus (2 Peter 1:8). Those who do not have these characteristics will live as though they've forgotten that "they have been cleansed from their past sins" (v. 9). These forgetful folks are the original selfies—self-centered, self-led, and self-powered slaves to sin.

Selfies give authority to the Enemy and allow his lies and labels of insufficiency to deceive them, discourage them, and even destroy them. Selfies remain shackled by shame for sins that have been washed away by the blood of Jesus. Selfies wrap themselves in a warped sense of identity defined by and tied to their temptations, their shame, their weaknesses, and their past sins. Selfies gird themselves with guilt, slinking around with sins that Christ freed them from the moment they accepted Him as Savior. Sometimes, selfies even minimize, justify, or glorify their sins of preference. Selfies will never experience true liberation until they die to self and receive the glorious gifts of grace, forgiveness, and life-transformation that are available to all who accept and honor Christ as Lord.

God's beloved image-bearers will have all the self-control we need to live holy lives *when* we surrender our self and our control to the Holy Spirit. Peter slammed a guarantee on the table: "If you do these things, you will never stumble, and you will receive a rich welcome into the eternal kingdom of our Lord and Savior Jesus Christ" (vv. 10–11). Demonstrating the value of loving leadership, the apostle committed to reminding the believers of these truths for as long as God allowed (vv. 12–15).

The development of our holiness is reliant on our faith in Jesus and our ongoing surrender to the Spirit. No matter what we've done or where God has brought us from, we can turn from temptation, repent of our sins, and live the righteous lives He intended for us. We can rejoice in our freedom from the sins that so easily entangled us and distorted our God-given identities. As Spirit-controlled servants, we can walk in the security, peace, hope, and liberation of His grace, obeying His Word one sacred stride at a time.

Inhale

> His divine power has given us everything we need for a godly life through our knowledge of him who called us by his own glory and goodness. (2 Peter 1:3)

Exhale

Shackle-breaking Spirit of God, thanks for freeing us from sin and giving us new lives through Christ. Empower us to leave our old lives behind and tie our identity to Jesus, not our temptations or past sins. Please give us all we need to live godly lives that lead others to a life-saving relationship with Jesus, through Your limitless power in us. Help us receive the liberation paid for on the cross by God the Son, as we submit to the loving authority of God the Father, and You produce an abundance of Your fruit in our lives. In Jesus's name, amen.

SACRED STRIDE

Ask the Holy Spirit to reveal any old-life declarations, any "I am" worldly mantras or labels based on your temptations, weaknesses, or past sins that you have accepted as core elements of your identity. Then ask Him to help you reject those lies so you can be a Spirit-controlled servant living a holy life of freedom and faith.

23

So Worth Loving

STEP INTO GOD'S WORD
Hebrews 10:19–25

STAND ON GOD'S TRUTH
*The Holy Spirit uses Scripture to affirm
that we are so worth loving.*

In March 2011, Eryn felt the Holy Spirit nudging her to start a lifestyle company to remind others they are worthy of love. God used her work to encourage people on over one hundred college campuses, in all fifty states, and in thirty-five countries. By 2016, Eryn had opened a storefront. However, while going through a divorce in 2018, she reached her burnout point and closed the store.

Emotionally and physically exhausted, she sank into depression. She had tried the good-Christian-girl life. She'd grown up in the church, met her husband at seventeen, and honored her purity commitment until she got married at twenty-one. As she grieved the loss of her nine-and-a-half-year marriage, Eryn felt punished and abandoned by God. She decided to live her truth, to do life her way. When things didn't work out, she lashed out at God. Still, desperate for relief, she read the passage of the day in her Bible app. Though the Holy Spirit used Scripture to assure her that He'd never punished or left her, Eryn remained skeptical. She longed to reclaim the promises she'd learned as a young girl but struggled with mistrust. She knew God would never force her to return, so she decided to test Him.

Eryn confessed her sins, vocalizing the things that brought her shame to see what God would think about her secrets. She bought a journal and wrote down all the things she'd done wrong. As she prayed over her list, wondering if God would still love her, she began to realize that her honesty was building her intimacy with Him.

She made small choices, slowly trusting Jesus, and allowed Him to be her Lord as she took baby steps of faith. Recognizing her fear of being vulnerable, Eryn asked the Holy Spirit to give her courage to continue journaling and holding nothing back. Though her problems didn't go away immediately, God remained true to His Word. He used other people to help and encourage Eryn. She eventually admitted that God already knew everything about her and all she'd done. He had just waited for her to be honest with Him and with herself.

As God affirmed His love for her, Eryn began falling in love with Him . . . again. She wrote down her confessions, repented, and asked for forgiveness daily. Her only goal was to talk to God consistently and ask what He thought about her. Though writing the bad stuff felt hard, writing the good stuff felt harder. Eventually the Holy Spirit helped her see that she was praising God whenever she wrote the good stuff. This process combated the Enemy's attempts to keep her focused on negativity and deepened her trust in God.

The more Eryn talked to God through journaling, the more she wanted to hear His voice. She began seriously studying the

Bible, and the Holy Spirit helped her approach Scripture differently while transforming her thinking. And the Scriptures, which had felt dead to her when she herself was dead inside, now felt alive as she pursued Jesus—and so did Eryn.

One day, she took small slips of paper and wrote down all the negative words people said to her, all the bad things she believed about herself. She stuck the lies on her mirror, then wrote the truth from Scripture on other slips of paper. Over time, God built a reservoir of trust that strengthened her confidence in her love relationship with Christ, deepened her compassion toward herself, and started changing how she lived in relationship to others. Now confident in God's love for her, she helps other women become more vulnerable with God, trusting He believes that they are so worth loving.

The ability to approach God honestly comes from the assurance of all Jesus has done on the cross, all He does to perfect our faith, and all He's promised to do. The writer of Hebrews wrote, "Since we have confidence to enter the Most Holy Place by the blood of Jesus, by a new and living way opened for us through the curtain, that is, his body, and since we have a great priest over the house of God, let us draw near to God with a sincere heart and with the full assurance that faith brings, having our hearts sprinkled to cleanse us from a guilty conscience and having our bodies washed with pure water" (Hebrews 10:19–22).

Our high priest, Jesus, abolished the need for a human intercessor, a person who serves as a mediator between us and God. Christ beckons us to draw nearer with vulnerability and stand in the sacred space of the holy of holies, God's presence, seeking to know Him intimately and trusting He knows us intimately. As we confess our sins and repent, assured of His grace, He affirms that we are forgiven and granted a new life.

We no longer need to succumb to the Enemy's temptations that hinder us from abundant life—for, the Spirit reminds us, we are forever freed and no longer defined by our sins. Our Creator and Sustainer has proven that we are so worth loving simply because we belong to Him.

The writer of Hebrews commissioned believers to take sacred strides with boldness together: "Let us hold unswervingly to the hope we profess, for he who promised is faithful. And let us consider how we may spur one another on toward love and good deeds, not giving up meeting together, as some are in the habit of doing, but encouraging one another—and all the more as you see the Day approaching" (vv. 23–25). That is the day of Christ's return, a day of rejoicing that proves the love of God is true. The day that fulfills prophecy.

On this side of eternity many will experience rejection and abuse, often because of their faith. However, we have everlasting hope built on the love Christ manifested through the cross. The Holy Spirit will enable us to believe the God-breathed words of Scripture, so we can know both God and ourselves as His image-bearers. Pouring His love into us, the Spirit ensures love overflows in our relationships with Him and others. His unerring truth negates the isolating, soul-destructing lies that don't align with His Word. With every sacred stride we take, we can know God thinks we are so worth loving. And so are the people He gives us the privilege to love as compassionately as He loves us.

Inhale

> Since we have a great High Priest who rules over God's house, let us go right into the presence of God with sincere hearts fully trusting him. (Hebrews 10:21–22 NLT)

Exhale

Worthy Spirit, thanks for giving us truth that negates the lies the Enemy has used to bind us to insecurities, shame, and guilt. Deepen our desire to prayerfully study Your Word so You can reveal truth that transforms us and sets us free. Give us courage to be honest with You and ourselves. And give us wisdom and strength to trust You, our unchanging God, not our ever-changing feelings. You are worthy of all our love, Lord. Thanks for assuring us that we are so worth loving simply because You love us. In Jesus's name, amen.

SACRED STRIDE

Ask the Holy Spirit to help you

- identify things you've done, thought, or believed that were against God's Word.
- repent, ask for forgiveness, and trust His grace is sufficient.
- search for Bible verses that affirm your purpose and value as God's image-bearer.
- trust that God thinks you and everyone He places in your life are so worth loving.

24

Prepared to Fight

STEP INTO GOD'S WORD
Ephesians 6:10–20

STAND ON GOD'S TRUTH
*The Holy Spirit maintains our spiritual
armor and fights on our behalf.*

I had my first fist fight in third grade. After my friend Becky finished chemo treatments, a girl named Margaret snatched Becky's cap off her bald head and teased her. When Becky ran away crying, a teacher caught me punching Margaret in the face. The principal gave me a "hack," a spanking with a wooden paddle as a form of corporal punishment. When he sent me home, I didn't even cry. My father had taught me to never back down from a fight or come home crying. My mother called me the strong one, the fighter in the family. So I kept my fighting spirit no matter what the consequences.

When I was twenty-one years old, almost a decade before I surrendered my life to Jesus, the consequences of my fighting spirit changed my life forever. A few friends and I went to a restaurant for a girls' night out. One of my friends rejected a man's advances as she walked across the crowded parking lot. He grabbed her by the hair, shoved her against a nearby car, and started choking her.

Without hesitation or considering the risks, I ran to help her. I couldn't pull the assailant off her, so I hit him in the back of the head once before his friend knocked me out with a fist to my face. I blacked out briefly while on the ground, then saw a bloody boot stomping on my friend's face. I crawled to her, shielded her head with my body, and took the brunt of the attacker's kicks on my back. As sirens rang in the distance, both assailants fled the scene. My friend and I lay bleeding and bruised on the ground, surrounded by people who had not stepped in to fight for us.

After my physical wounds healed, I kept looking over my shoulder, always anxious, angry, and afraid. When my cousin Rosie invited me to stay with her and her family, over an hour away from that parking lot, I accepted her offer but insisted I was fine. I met my husband while living with my cousin. I didn't know it then, but one of the reasons I married him was because he made me feel safe.

I don't remember when my husband and I started sparring with words that cut deep, left scars, and destroyed that safe-space feeling. After we'd been together for a decade, I had no fight left in me. But I didn't know how to stop fighting, either. As my marriage unraveled, and after a three-month separation, I took our sons to a local church. I surrendered my life to Jesus in December 2001 and began reading the Bible.

The Holy Spirit handled my heart gently as He healed one wound at a time and helped me believe one promise at a time. He revealed my true enemy and used Scripture to teach me a new way of sparring on the real battlefield, the spiritual realm. As I prayed, He assured me that His way of fighting would make me thrive, not just barely survive.

Over time, God helped me discern that my fighting spirit was a defense mechanism rooted in fear and insecurity caused by childhood trauma. He anchored me in His love and used the life-giving and life-changing words of Scripture to transform my thinking and my character. He gave me the courage to be vulnerable, the strength to admit my weaknesses, and the wisdom to talk and pray about my struggles with Him and within a safe fellowship of believers. God's still working on me and my relationships.

More importantly, the Holy Spirit showed me I could access His power by calling on Him, trusting His reliability, and submitting to Him one breath at a time. Though fear and insecurity still sometimes tempt me to clench my fists, the Holy Spirit enables me to open my palms and surrender as I inhale His truth and exhale prayers and praises. Through this open line of communication, He returns my focus to my Father's business—fulfilling the Great Commission while living out the Greatest Commandment. He doesn't just give me strength or help me feel safe; the Holy Spirit is my strength and my safe space.

In Ephesians 6, the apostle Paul urged the believers to "be strong in the Lord and in his mighty power" (v. 10). Their true source of strength could not be accessed apart from the Lord. Being strong in Him requires us to acknowledge His constant presence and power, relying on Him for everything.

Paul continued, "Put on the full armor of God, so that you can take your stand against the devil's schemes" (v. 11). The devil, wrote the apostle Peter, is our true adversary, who "prowls around like a roaring lion looking for someone to devour" (1 Peter 5:8). Since the devil will always be scheming, believers will always be under spiritual attack. Paul therefore urged them to be intentional about employing their God-given armor—because their "struggle is not against flesh and blood, but against the rulers, against the authorities, against the powers of this dark world and against the spiritual forces of evil in the heavenly realms" (Ephesians 6:12).

Fellow image-bearers are not a believer's true enemies. They are mere pawns used by the Enemy to wreak havoc. Paul describes the lifelong war, the real battlefield, the believers' status as victors through Christ, and their continuous need for God's power and protection. "Put on the full armor of God," he told the Ephesians—and tells us—"so that when the day of evil comes, you may be able to stand your ground, and after you have done everything, to stand" (v. 13). Combat with evil is inevitable, so believers always need spiritual intervention.

"Stand firm then, with the belt of truth buckled around your waist, with the breastplate of righteousness in place, and with your feet fitted with the readiness that comes from the gospel of peace" (vv. 14–15). The belt, breastplate, and boots of faith work together. Considering that Jesus proclaims *He* is the way, the truth, and the life, the belt of truth could be described as the most intimate protection of a Christian: a life girded by a personal relationship with Jesus, "the pioneer and perfector of our faith" (Hebrews 12:2).

God provides the breastplate of righteousness to shield and strengthen the core and most vital organ of a believer's physical and spiritual being, the heart. Proverbs 4:23 tells us to guard the heart "with all vigilance, for from it flow the springs of life" (ESV). Treasuring God's Word in our hearts, not just our minds, enables us to avoid sinning against Him (Psalm 119:11). Our hearts are also intricately involved in solidifying our faith. Paul said, "If you declare with your mouth, 'Jesus is Lord,' and believe in your heart that God raised him from the dead, you will be saved. For it is with your heart that you believe and are justified, and it is with your mouth that you profess your faith and are saved" (Romans 10:9–10).

As we believe and live according to the Scriptures, God will lead us to bring peace to the world (v. 15). His peacemakers don't need to fight like warriors of the world, though. We fight from a place of victory because we know we've already won the war through Christ. Therefore, we can confidently "take up the shield of faith," or trust, and live like we believe God gives us power to "extinguish all the flaming arrows of the evil one" (Ephesians 6:16). Jesus's identity as God the Son—His attributes, His promises, His sacrifice, His resurrection, His life—is the shield of our faith.

Paul charged the believers to "pray in the Spirit on all occasions with all kinds of prayers and requests. With this in mind, be alert and always keep on praying for all the Lord's people" (v. 18). Individual and intercessory prayer are the Christian's lifeline and war cry. We need God and each other as we fight spiritual battles. The Enemy lives on borrowed time under God-given limitations and without omniscience or power over God's people. When we pray, we are immediately accessing the power of God in us. We can pray and praise Him with every breath we take when we're walking by faith on the holy ground of His constant presence. As we wave the white flag of surrender to the Holy Spirit, we can fight the good fight. With a victory stance, we can live each moment in submission to Christ as our almighty Lord, our holy King, and our living God forever.

Inhale

> Finally, be strong in the Lord and in his mighty power. (Ephesians 6:10)

Exhale

Mighty and merciful Spirit of God, thanks for fighting for us and for those who have yet to experience the victory of a life submitted under Your authority. Make us fierce warriors in spiritual battle, armed with confident prayers and grateful praises of expectant faith. Empower us to submit to You and fight Your way. Please give us the courage we need to embrace our weaknesses, confess and turn from our sins, and trust You are our strength and safe space. In Jesus's name, amen.

SACRED STRIDE

Join me for one of the most powerful spiritual growth adventures you will ever experience. Visit www.odbm.org and subscribe to the free devotionals. No matter how you choose to receive them, they all include a Bible-in-a-year reading plan.

A Celebration Place

STEP INTO GOD'S WORD
1 John 3:1–24

STAND ON GOD'S TRUTH
*The Holy Spirit helps us celebrate and love
all our beautifully diverse neighbors.*

In 1995, God led Dorena and her husband to Franklin, Tennessee, to start a diverse church committed to loving their neighbors, discipleship, and the expansion of God's kingdom. In 2013, God changed their meeting place. Amid streets named for Civil War heroes in Nashville, the Holy Spirit empowered the African American pastor and his family to lead and love a congregation of people across cultural, social, and generational lines. Some people left when God moved the church. With those losses came struggles with finances and staff changes. Often misunderstood and overcome with despair and distrust, Dorena felt like she was crawling by faith. The Enemy tried to deceive her into thinking all she did was worthless.

But during that transitional season, God worked in and through Dorena and her church family. He used her experiences to deepen her desire to share what the church could be—what it's supposed to be—as His image-bearers do life together.

Dorena celebrated how God was building a diverse community under her and her husband's leadership. But the growing pains often stirred up deep emotions and tension within the congregation. After the murder of Trayvon Martin, Dorena reflected on the pain of Black parents raising their children to be confident in their skin. Yet, some brothers and sisters in Christ were raising their children to be color-blind. Dorena struggled with the concept. Color blindness requires people to be unseen, which is not God's way or His design for the church. Pretending to not see color is counterproductive and unbiblical. So Dorena asked God how He wanted her to respond.

As Dorena prayed for the church, the Holy Spirit stirred up her passion to create what she couldn't give her children: picture books that honored her Christian values *and* included diverse characters. Dorena proceeded to write her stories and researched the various options for publication. She had no agent, no writing community, no platform or extended reach. After a year of rejections, she prayed and placed the stories on a shelf. Just as Dorena was ready to quit, God sent a friend to introduce her to an acquiring agent at a publishing house. Eighteen months later, Dorena released her first children's book. Her fourth children's book, published in 2021, proclaims that the church is a celebration place and includes illustrations reflecting the diverse congregation at her own church.

Empowering people to love involves sharing hard historical truths people have minimized, ignored, and distorted. In 2022, Dorena released a board book about Juneteenth. June 19, 1865, is the day the enslaved people in Galveston, Texas, finally found out the Civil War had ended and they were free. This happened two years *after* President Abraham

Lincoln issued the Emancipation Proclamation, which ended slavery in America. Dorena's story of Juneteenth has become a conversation starter and a resource for children and adults. Readers are learning about Juneteenth and discovering that loving others requires willingness to face the uncomfortable, sad, and unjust moments in history. As Dorena continues writing, God is using her books to start vital conversations, change lives, build relationships, and equip His children of all ages to celebrate and love their beautifully diverse neighbors around the world.

In 1 John 3, the apostle proclaimed, "See what great love the Father has lavished on us, that we should be called children of God!" (v. 1). God's love is the foundation on which He builds His family. John continued, "This is how we know who the children of God are and who the children of the devil are: Anyone who does not do what is right is not God's child, nor is anyone who does not love their brother and sister" (v. 10). Whoever does not love all God's image-bearers does not love God. And racism, colorism, prejudice, biases, and perpetuating stereotypes are not loving. When we reject our God-given diversity and refuse inclusion, equity, and justice for all, we fail to love.

Just like God's plan for a diverse church has never changed, His plan for a loving church has never changed. "For this is the message you heard from the beginning: We should love one another" (v. 11). John took the believers back to the first act of hatred in the Bible as an example. He said believers should not be like Cain, "who belonged to the evil one and murdered his brother. And why did he murder him? Because his own actions were evil and his brother's were righteous" (vv. 12–13). Cain couldn't love his brother because Abel's righteousness shone a light on his wickedness. Though the apostle John was

155

referring to relationships between the believers in these verses, God desires for our love to flow in the church and into every relationship outside the church. This is the way the church can thrive and grow.

John correlated being unloving with being dead (v. 14) and even went a step further: "Anyone who hates a brother or sister is a murderer, and you know that no murderer has eternal life residing in him" (v. 15). Strong and uncomfortable words, yes, but they express God's love for the world Jesus died for, the people He does not want to perish. This includes not only the people who love Him but even those who reject Him. However, loving Jesus and loving like Jesus are countercultural, and often provoke the hatred of those who reject God and His command to love, in the church and outside of the church.

God takes love seriously. In Matthew 5, Jesus said that "anyone who is angry with a brother or sister will be subject to judgment" (v. 22). He also said we should love our enemies (Matthew 5:43–44). First Corinthians 13, commonly called the Bible's "love chapter," describes love in depth. And John, with fewer words, points to love's ultimate display: "This is how we know what love is: Jesus Christ laid down his life for us. And we ought to lay down our lives for our brothers and sisters" (1 John 3:16). While again this verse refers to believers, God's Word commands love without boundaries or exceptions. And that love is more than just talk or goodwill. It's a practical love, impacting the lives of God's diverse, uniquely created image-bearers. In John's words, "If anyone has material possessions and sees a brother or sister in need but has no pity on them, how can the love of God be in that person? Dear children, let us not love with words or speech but with actions and in truth" (vv. 17–18).

Love doesn't judge, reject people who are different, or try

to fix people until they accept or obey God. We're simply to love people, share the gospel, and invest in their lives so we can all be transformed by the life-changing love of Christ. Love doesn't allow us to live in bubbles with people who resemble us or agree with us all the time. If we look around and see that everyone in our personal sphere of influence is similar to us, we're missing the mark of loving like Jesus. How can we be lights that point to Jesus if we refuse to leave the sanctuary and serve our communities, or if we don't allow people from our communities to enter the sanctuary and meet Jesus?

Let's celebrate and love all the people God loves. Let's *be* the safe space that invites all God's image-bearers to hear the gospel. The Spirit can use God's love flowing through us to point others to a life-changing relationship with Jesus, so they can encounter God's love personally and experience freedom from sin. After all, God is love, and His vision for the church has never changed. Love can, however, change our perception of the people God made and loves so that His church will truly be a celebration place.

Inhale

This is the message you heard from the beginning: We should love one another. (1 John 3:11)

Exhale

Uniting and loving Spirit of God, thanks for creating a world filled with diverse people whom You love completely. Please make us secure in how You created us so that we can have the confidence to celebrate the way You created others. Help us build authentic relationships with people who are different from us. Help us listen to learn, so we can love others with our words, our actions, and our thoughts. Show us how You want us to live generously, love selflessly, and stand for justice, equity, and inclusion while leading others to a lifesaving relationship with You through the heart-changing love of Christ. In Jesus's name, amen.

SACRED STRIDE

Ask the Holy Spirit to reveal any personal biases and prejudices that have hindered you from loving all your neighbors as wonderfully and marvelously created image-bearers. Then ask Him to help you build authentic relationships with people who are different from you so the church can truly be a celebration place.

26

Everlasting Hope

STEP INTO GOD'S WORD
John 14:15–31

STAND ON GOD'S TRUTH
The Holy Spirit fills our hope tanks in the
refuge of His constant presence.

When Beth was thirteen, having accepted Jesus in middle school, she trusted God after her parents divorced. At sixteen, her mother gave her permission to get married. Randy was good to her. Yet Beth struggled with intimacy. She felt alone, insignificant, and unworthy of care or compassion.

God used Randy to help heal Beth's wounded heart. He was the only person who believed her when she accused her biological father of molesting her. Still, her toxic paternal relationship influenced the way Beth viewed relationships with all men.

While working with a counselor, Beth asked God to help her develop a healthy view of intimacy. Though she never felt betrayed by God, she struggled with saying she had an "intimate relationship" with Him. She didn't want to call God her Father, especially when she thought about the things her earthly father did to her. The word *intimate* felt wrong and triggered emotions from the trauma she had experienced. But the Holy Spirit gave Beth peace when she decided to refer to intimacy with God as "a close or deeper relationship with the Lord."

As Beth continued working on how she related to God, Randy, and their two sons, she read her Bible and daily devotions consistently. The Holy Spirit spoke through Scripture and those who taught Scripture. One day a pastor's message nudged Beth to forgive her father. As she prayed, she wrote him a letter of forgiveness. Two years later, after her earthly father died, Beth thanked her heavenly Father for giving her peace and closure.

When a complicated domestic dispute led to the murder of Randy's cousin, Beth's beloved husband turned to drinking. He isolated himself and refused counseling. She prayed and attended a support group for people affected by someone else's alcoholism. Eventually, grieving, she took her sons and divorced Randy.

Adjusting to her new life as a divorcée proved challenging. Depleted by the onslaught of hardships, Beth considered taking her own life. She felt the Holy Spirit stopping her and wrapping her in His enduring hope. God lavished Beth with joyful times with her sons, and eventually He brought a kind man into their lives. Joshua grew to love her sons as his own. But he was not a believer, and Beth prayed for his salvation. Eventually they got married.

Marriage made life no easier, though, especially after Beth's oldest son came home from the war in Iraq. The turmoil escalated on Mother's Day in 2020, when, in front of Beth, he tried to kill his dog, then threatened to shoot himself. Beth tried to calm him down and prayed for help. She understood that her soldier son, suffering from the horrid ramifications of post-traumatic stress disorder and numerous traumatic brain injuries, would never recover this side of heaven, but he was learning how to adapt.

Alone with her son in the house at the time, afraid, but trusting that God was with her, Beth texted her Bible study group, asking for intercessory prayer.

As Beth prayed silently, her son pointed his gun at her. She saw the torment in his eyes. Then he threw the gun away and called a family friend. And Beth, after locking herself in her bedroom, reached out to the military crisis line. She felt the Holy Spirit with her every moment.

God continued to work in Beth's life, as well as her son's, as He worked to heal their relationship. Though the hardships continued, and Beth often struggled, the Holy Spirit helped her face each new day with gratitude for all He had done and hope as she witnessed what He was doing. God used others, especially her husband and youngest son, and the Scriptures to comfort and strengthen Beth. He reminded her that her peace rested on His steady presence, not changeable circumstances. Lovingly, God encouraged Beth with nuggets of beauty in the world He created.

Yet concern for her husband's salvation continued to weigh heavily on Beth's heart. Finally, in 2023, it came to a head. In response to Beth's heartfelt prayers, God broke through—and Joshua surrendered his life to Jesus.

Jesus said His followers would have troubles in this world, but our hope would be secure because He had overcome the world (John 16:33). God has also always promised His presence and provided peace and hope for His image-bearers, but not without conditions. In John 14, Jesus said to the disciple, "If you love me, keep my commands. And I will ask the Father, and he will give you another advocate to help you and be with you forever—the Spirit of truth" (vv. 15–17). As Jesus prepared to fulfill His purpose on Calvary, He promised the disciples that the Holy Spirit, the third person of the Godhead, would be their ever-present helper. Nonbelievers wouldn't know or understand Him, but the Spirit would be with and in those who accepted Christ as their Savior and Lord.

Jesus said, "Before long, the world will not see me anymore, but you will see me. Because I live, you also will live" (v. 19). Jesus assured His followers they would be serving a living God. Jesus died a physical death on the cross at Calvary as an atoning sacrifice, paying the wages of our sins in full. Then, defeating death, He rose in victory as the risen King.

The disciples couldn't know what the next Pentecost, soon to come, would mean for them. But the Lord did. He said, "On that day you will realize that I am in my Father, and you are in me, and I am in you" (v. 20). After they received the Holy Spirit, He would help them understand and live according to the Scriptures. He would help them believe and preach the good news. Inspired by the Spirit of God, the disciples would write what we now know as the New Testament—which He has protected and preserved through the millennia.

Jesus said the disciples would demonstrate genuine love for Him through their obedience (vv. 21–24). And He promised them, "All this I have spoken while still with you. But the Advocate, the Holy Spirit, whom the Father will send in my name, will teach you all things and will remind you of everything I have said to you" (vv. 25–26). This beautiful proclamation supports the doctrine of the Trinity: the Son said the Father would send the Spirit to be the Advocate the disciples would need to fulfill their God-given purpose in life. And the Spirit would teach the disciples "all things," reflected in the entire canon of the Bible we know today.

Jesus understood what the disciples would face. He knew they would need the Holy Spirit. Only the Spirit of God could bring

Jesus's words to mind and strengthen their resolve when they became weary or completely wiped out. Acknowledging their human frailty, Jesus said, "Peace I leave with you; my peace I give you. I do not give to you as the world gives. Do not let your hearts be troubled and do not be afraid" (v. 27). Jesus's peace, *shalom*, would remain unshakable in all circumstances. His *shalom* would withstand their bouts with doubt, discouragement, and despair.

Then, following the promise of His second coming (v. 28), Jesus assured the disciples that the "prince of this world," the Enemy, the already defeated Father of Lies, had "no hold over" Him (v. 30). The Enemy's desperate attempts to destroy God's children only reveal the extensiveness of Jesus's love for the Father (v. 31). The Enemy knows Jesus's identity and His status as the King who will come again. The liar also knows the Father has provided a limited time to stir up chaos in this world. So the Deceiver fights fiercely and unfairly, though he has no power or authority over any believer. Followers of Christ can walk by faith because we have God the Spirit dwelling in us. The Holy Spirit empowers and encourages disciples of Christ until the day we are called home to heaven or until Jesus returns.

When we accept Jesus as our Savior and Lord, we receive the Holy Spirit in that moment and become children of God with everlasting hope. The Holy Spirit will not leave us for one millisecond. The living God was, and is, and always will be God with us and in us.

Inhale

The Advocate, the Holy Spirit, whom the Father will send in my name, will teach you all things and will remind you of everything I have said to you. (John 14:26)

Exhale

Persistent Helper, thanks for using the unerring words of Scripture to encourage and empower us no matter what we're facing. Thanks for affirming that we can expect Your mercy and power to carry us through trials one sacred step at a time or, when necessary, one sacred breath at a time. Give us a desire to connect with You through constant prayer, to study Your Word, and to submit to the authority of Your Word. Change us, Spirit of God. Make us more like Jesus as You give us opportunities to share Your Word with others who need Your everlasting hope just as much as we do. In Jesus's name, amen.

SACRED STRIDE

Say fingertip prayers out loud or silently by touching the tip of each finger:

1. The thumb points to you. Ask the Spirit to deepen your relationship with God.
2. The forefinger points to others. Pray for family members and friends.
3. The middle finger extends further. Pray for the global church.
4. The ring finger inspires commitment. Pray for your church family and the local community you serve.
5. The pinky hooks to God's promises. Pray for people who don't know Jesus yet.

27

Strength in Surrender

STEP INTO GOD'S WORD
2 Corinthians 3:17–18 and 4:1–18

STAND ON GOD'S TRUTH
*The Holy Spirit empowers us to surrender so
He can align our strides with His.*

Alan was still recovering from his lower back surgery when we moved to Wisconsin in 2018. He continued physical therapy while serving as my full-time caregiver, adjusting to his new position, and teaching online classes. The brutal weather took its toll on us. And we took out our frustrations on each other, even before the pandemic. When my health declined, Alan's responsibility as a caregiver got harder. He had to rely on the Holy Spirit like never before to help him keep trusting and following God. We believed going home would make life easier, so we prayed as Alan applied for jobs in the Bay Area. When he didn't get immediate results, though, Alan felt like God was not answering his prayers.

Finally, in September 2020, God said yes to our request. However, getting what we asked for—a job for Alan that allowed us to return home—did not lead where we expected. We had to stay in a hotel for over a month before we found an apartment, but it was on the third floor with no elevator. Frustrated and determined to save for a house, Alan began teaching more online classes. In March 2021, God blessed us with a brand-new home under the budget we had planned for a fixer-upper. We prayed and praised God on the dirt lot for this unexpected and much-needed chance to exhale.

A few months later, however, Alan's boss informed him that his interim position would not lead into the full-time position he was promised. After receiving his last check in June, Alan leaned into God as his unemployment put us at risk of losing our loan for the house.

The Holy Spirit reminded Alan of what he'd learned in the Bible and kept bringing Psalm 27:14 to his mind: "Wait for the LORD; be strong and take heart and wait for the LORD." So Alan prayed, and in November God provided an even better job.

Before we could finish praising God, one blow after another hit us hard. My service dog had surgery on her back foot, and Alan tore his Achilles tendon while carrying Callie down the steps. From that day on, every step Alan took caused excruciating pain. He persevered at work and at home, but life's circumstances kept battering him. In the first week of January 2022, he had dental surgery, a cancer scare, and strained vocal cords. The following week, I was hospitalized. With decreased mobility and increased pain, I moved in with our son Xavier and his fiancé Arriana because I could no longer handle steps. Alan stayed in our apartment alone.

In 2022, we officially welcomed our daughter-in-love, Arriana, into the family with a trip to Hawaii. Xavier helped us move into our new home. And we rejoiced over the birth of our grandson, Xarian. But Alan also had surgery on his

Achilles in February, an endoscopy in March, and rotator cuff surgery in June.

In 2023, a partial knee replacement in February required a second surgery in March. In 2024, Xavier and Arri blessed us with our granddaughter, Xaria. Though still working full-time and serving as my caregiver while experiencing high levels of pain, Alan stepped in as the facilitator of an online prayer group. In September, still trying to catch his breath and manage everything, Alan had a full knee replacement on the same knee. He had carpal tunnel surgery on December 26, 2024, and began preparing for a second full knee replacement to be scheduled in 2025, the fourth surgery on his left knee in two years.

Alan was tired.

He couldn't read his Bible regularly. He didn't like receiving help from others outside our family. Buckling under the mounting pressures, we jabbed at each other with hurtful words, blaming and complaining. I asked God to work on our hearts and help my husband experience His unconditional love and abounding grace.

I praised God when I saw Alan reading Scripture regularly again in January 2025. The thought of God's past faithfulness and how much God loved him despite his shortcomings overwhelmed Alan. Still limping while recovering from his fifteenth surgery, Alan prayed for spiritual healing and strength. He had to rely on God completely.

God has a history of using people who know they are unable to do anything without Him. In 2 Corinthians 3, the apostle Paul wrote, "Now the Lord is the Spirit, and where the Spirit of the Lord is, there is freedom. And we all, who with unveiled faces contemplate the Lord's glory, are being transformed into his image with ever-increasing glory, which comes from the Lord, who is the Spirit" (vv. 17–18). The Holy Spirit's presence in the life of a believer results in freedom, not bondage. Surrendering to the Spirit brings life, not death. "Therefore, since through God's mercy we have this ministry, we do not lose heart" (2 Corinthians 4:1).

The Holy Spirit enables us to follow Him and persevere in a world filled with affliction, a world in which many refuse to accept Scripture as always right, relevant, and life-changing (vv. 2–3). Paul said, "The god of this age has blinded the minds of unbelievers, so that they cannot see the gospel that displays the glory of Christ, who is the image of God" (v. 4). Though this is true, Christ followers can still share the gospel through the power of the Holy Spirit (v. 5). "For God, who said, 'Let light shine out of darkness,' made his light shine in our hearts to give us the light of the knowledge of God's glory displayed in the face of Christ" (v. 6).

Paul acknowledged the weakness of God's image-bearers and the eternal value of the magnificent treasure that is the gospel. He said, "This all-surpassing power is from God and not from us" (v. 7). The apostle realized the importance of recognizing our weaknesses so we can understand our desperate need for God and His promise of abundant grace. Paul said of the bearers and sharers of the gospel, which should be all believers in Jesus, "We are hard pressed on every side, but not crushed; perplexed, but not in despair; persecuted, but not abandoned; struck down, but not destroyed" (vv. 8–9). Since God's people are victorious in the end, we're also victors in the present, no matter how battle-worn our armor has become.

Though we walk by faith through an ongoing spiritual battle, our enduring strength comes through persevering submission to the Spirit and our everlasting hope in Christ (vv. 10–14). God brings us through trials, molding our testimonies as the Spirit deepens our faith and uses us as beacons of hope. "All this is for your benefit, so that the grace that is reaching more and more people may cause thanksgiving to overflow to the glory of God" (v. 15).

God doesn't limit our end goal to this world. When we place our trust in Christ, our hope is not determined by what we can see or what we're experiencing. "Therefore we do not lose heart. Though outwardly we are wasting away, yet inwardly we are being renewed day by day. For our light and momentary troubles are achieving for us an eternal glory that far outweighs them all. So we fix our eyes not on what is seen, but on what is unseen, since what is seen is temporary, but what is unseen is eternal" (vv. 16–18).

We may not recognize God's "no" of protection until years later or sometimes not at all. However, as we trust God's way with every breath we take, we will discover we are strongest when we surrender to Him. We can submit to the ever-present Spirit of God and face uncertainties and trials with supernatural peace, joy, hope, and even gratitude for the blessing of seeing Him work in and through our lives for His glory. As we release everything into His trustworthy hands, we will recognize God's personal answers to our prayers are always a manifestation of His tender, loving care in our lives.

Inhale

> We have this treasure in jars of clay to show that this all-surpassing power is from God and not from us.
> (2 Corinthians 4:7)

Exhale

Tender, loving Spirit, when our faith wanes and trials feel relentless, thanks for assuring us that You will care for us completely.

Give us a hunger to communicate with You through prayer, even when those prayers are simply silent tears, indiscernible groans, or exhalations of weariness. Help us seek Your wisdom in the Scriptures, even if we can only manage a small taste. Increase our trust so we will seek Your direction and submit to Your will. Then, help us to rest in Your presence, as we rely on Your power and receive Your yes and Your no with gratitude and confidence in Your love and grace. In Jesus's name, amen.

SACRED STRIDE

(If you have physical health concerns, consult your doctor before you begin the following.)
Find a safe space to sit in silence and breathe slowly. Then . . .

1. Clench your fists and contemplate God the Father's love for you.
2. With fists remaining clenched, spread your arms out to the side and thank God the Son for the cross.
3. Tighten your fists, inhale deeply, and acknowledge God the Spirit's presence.
4. Exhale slowly and say "Hallelujah!" as you open your fists quickly.
5. Raise your open palms over your head and say, "Holy Spirit, I am Yours. Do what You will."
6. Lower your arms and ask God to show you the next sacred stride He wants you to take.

Repeat as often as you like.

28

Worshiping Warrior

STEP INTO GOD'S WORD
Psalm 145

STAND ON GOD'S TRUTH
The Holy Spirit is all we need to live as worshiping warriors.

In April 2020, shortly before the pandemic shut down the world, doctors confirmed that Lara's son, Sol, had Duchenne muscular dystrophy. This genetic disease, a severe form of muscular dystrophy that affects boys primarily, causes progressive muscle pain and degeneration, often leads to liver and heart failure, and greatly reduces life expectancy. While Lara's husband, Wes, served on the front lines as a nurse, Lara grieved at home alone with Sol and his older sister, Addy. She told God that she was angry with Him. She didn't feel like reading His Word or hearing about His sovereign goodness. He parted the Red Sea. He did miracles in the Bible. He could heal her son. So why didn't He?

Deep down, Lara knew Sol's diagnosis wasn't God's fault. She believed He heard her prayers. Still, at times, Lara really wanted to blame God. She would often be singing out loud before realizing she was worshiping God. But for a year, she would not touch her Bible.

The family moved into a house they could remodel for wheelchair accessibility, which kept Lara busy. One day, as she watched her children playing quietly in their finished basement, Lara noticed that Addy helped Sol without being asked. She excelled at encouraging and snuggling him. The Holy Spirit assured Lara that Addy was the perfect big sister for Sol.

Suddenly, four-year-old Sol stood up in the middle of the room and sang out loud, "Praise the Lord God! Praise the Lord God!" Turning to Lara, who had captured the moment on video, Sol shrugged and went back to playing with his sister. Seeing someone so small singing with such big faith humbled Lara.

One day, Sol told Lara he did not want to use a wheelchair. But to get around without one, he would need a service dog. So I introduced them to my service dog's trainer. We started a fundraiser for Sol in June 2020, and in September, days before God moved us from Wisconsin back to California, we met our goal. People in the community and online from around the world raised $22,000, which covered the costs of a puppy and the two-year service dog training program. In 2023, Waffles joined Lara's family. While Tails for Life would continue custom training as Sol's needs changed, Waffles's main tasks would be to help Sol with balance, retrieve items, and give plenty of cuddles. Waffles would also keep Sol out of the wheelchair for as long as possible.

Lara began dreaming of an all-inclusive playground that all students could safely enjoy, a playground where children with and without disabilities could foster genuine friendships. Advocating for a better quality of life for Sol and other children with disabilities in their community, Lara joined a fundraiser to raise $400,000 for an all-inclusive playground at Sol's elementary school. They raised $36,000 by the end of 2023, but Lara didn't receive the support she expected from the community or the district. Though disappointed, she praised God. She understood that their hope was secured in Christ, not Sol's diagnosis or a playground where he could enjoy being a kid with his friends. As Lara clung to the fact that there is no Duchenne's in heaven, she continued praying expectantly for a cure.

In 2024, Lara and Wes enjoyed their fifteenth anniversary. They celebrated Addy's tenth birthday and Sol's eighth birthday. They rejoiced as Waffles started going to school with Sol in September. And they praised God when their local school district received a generous donation from a community business which, accompanied by the district's funding, would build new playgrounds in nine schools.

A few months later, however, Lara realized the plans did not include inclusive equipment. She prayed as she communicated her concerns with the school district, offering her research and the money they'd raised. When she was told to stop fundraising and accept the proposed playground with a few accessible pieces of equipment or her son's school would not receive a new playground at all, Lara lamented. Considering the other students, she trusted God would provide as He always had and praised Him for the equipment they would receive.

In November Sol's school finally had one of the most all-inclusive playgrounds in the district, though its accessibility was moderate. When Lara saw students with and without disabilities playing on the few all-inclusive structures, the Holy Spirit filled her with compassion for the other schools in her district and in other communities that did not have accessible playgrounds. And, in December 2024, she committed to keep fighting for her son and praying for a world where people with and without disabilities can play, work, and serve Jesus together.

Through Sol, the Holy Spirit reminds Lara to appreciate the life they've been given, even when the road ahead feels too long and too hard. Knowing she may have to bury her son, Lara asks God to help her be present with Him, her husband, and her children. Her tiny but mighty worshiping warrior has inspired Lara to read her Bible again and sing on her church's worship team. She rests in the surety of God's love, which she has experienced in countless ways. Her whole family knows He is worthy to be praised.

David began Psalm 145 with a public proclamation and a prayer: "I will exalt you, my God the King; I will praise your name for ever and ever. Every day I will praise you and extol your name for ever and ever" (vv. 1–2). Focusing on God's character and actions—on what David had seen and experienced, not just heard about God—he sang, "Great is the LORD and most worthy of praise; his greatness no one can fathom" (v. 3). The psalmist celebrated the far-reaching majesty of God, the intimate, relevant, and life-changing grandness of God's reputation, which would be passed down generation to generation (v. 4). David honored corporate and personal worship as he sang, "They speak of the glorious splendor of your majesty—and I will meditate on your wonderful works" (v. 5). He would not be the only one who would celebrate God's abundant goodness and righteousness while testifying about all God had done, all God was doing, and all God promised to do (vv. 6–7).

Acknowledging God's merciful patience, the psalmist sang, "The LORD is gracious and compassionate, slow to anger and rich in love" (v. 8). Based on his personal interactions with God, David saw God's heart for all His image-bearers: "The LORD is good to all; he has compassion on all he has made" (v. 9).

With his declaration of God's grandness, David seemed to recognize the power of personal testimonies. One purpose for praising God was so all people might know of His "mighty acts and the glorious splendor of [His] kingdom" (v. 12). David sang of God's dominion, His trustworthiness and faithfulness as a promise keeper, His continual help and sustaining power as the One who "lifts up all who are bowed down" (vv. 13–14). With the heart song of a worshiping warrior filled with big faith, David extolled God's generous provision of food for "every living thing" (vv. 15–16). The Lord, David proclaimed, is continually attentive "to all who call on him in truth" (v. 18).

"[God] fulfills the desires of those who fear him"—who revere Him, who stand in awe of Him—and "he hears their cry and saves them" (v. 19). Even when grief, sorrow, or affliction has hunched our shoulders over with lament, our trust in the heart of God can lead us into a space of contentment until His compassion has carried us through our trials. For He is ever watchful and just (v. 20). The Holy Spirit is all we need to live, like David, as worshiping warriors who sing together: "My mouth will speak in praise of the LORD. Let every creature praise his holy name for ever and ever" (v. 21). To God be the glory, the honor, and the praise, praise, praise!

Inhale

> Great is the LORD and most worthy of praise;
>   his greatness no one can fathom.
> (Psalm 145:3)

Exhale

Never-changing Spirit of God, thanks for being compassionate with us when we're struggling and remaining faithful with the

175

unexpected, uncomfortable, and unwelcome changes in life. Remind us that our identities are not defined by the good or bad things that happen to us or the way others perceive or treat us. Thanks for confirming that we don't have to feel strong or have all we want before we can be worshiping warriors because You are our strength and all we need. Help us trust You will be who You say You are, and You'll be where You say You'll be—always with us. In Jesus's name, amen.

SACRED STRIDE

Ask the Holy Spirit to help you create a gratitude list. Use the following as your guide:

- I am grateful that God is (character traits or attributes).
- I am grateful that God has (things He has done for you— nothing is too small).
- I am grateful that God will (promises He will keep).

Then, close your eyes and sing your favorite worship song out loud, without caring about who is listening or how you sound.

Freed!

STEP INTO GOD'S WORD
Colossians 3:1–17

STAND ON GOD'S TRUTH
The Holy Spirit frees us so that we can serve Him from a place of healing, holiness, and hope.

After I received Jesus as my Savior, I didn't know how to accept Him as the ruler with authority over every aspect of my life. I believed the gospel and desperately wanted to claim the freedom Christ offered me. But I wasn't even sure I *could* submit to Christ. I ran away from my earthly parents at fifteen and only had a relationship with my mom, which thankfully improved when I became an adult. When I surrendered my life to Jesus at thirty, as an older new Christian, I expected my heavenly Father to treat me like the people He created had treated me. My past experiences taught me that I needed to provide for myself and protect myself. And when I couldn't, I simply did my best to survive. I excelled at shielding my heart with anger, false confidence, and apathy, until I was alone with my thoughts. I didn't feel forgiven or free.

As I learned to study Scripture within its context, I began

comparing myself to Jesus instead of comparing myself to other sinners like me. I knew that I was not a *good* person just because someone else was worse than me. I fell short every day. I even stole my first Bible from a church. However, after I started prayerfully reading and studying the God-breathed words of Scripture for familiarity each year, I became like a giddy schoolgirl, excited to know God and make Him known as He transformed me.

I still reach for that stolen-but-now-paid-in-full Bible sometimes. I read the highlighted and underlined verses. I praise God as I skim the study notes, prayers, and praises written in the margins. Each one is a testimony of how the Holy Spirit worked and is working in and through my life. Still, even as God changed me and led me to share His Word with others, I often struggled to accept that His truth applied to *me*. The Holy Spirit helped me recognize that by holding on to old lies, I was placing myself before God. I was living as if God and His Word were insufficient and irrelevant.

As time passed, God revealed that my self-centeredness kept me from the life-giving freedom Christ offered and the genuine community I needed and desired. When the Holy Spirit breaks through years of bondage, He begins by using a mirror to reveal the greatest obstacle to living the abundant life Jesus promises His disciples. To experience freedom in Christ—freedom that cannot be hindered by chains, walls, bars, or hardened hearts—I had to stop striving for self-preservation.

I went through the Celebrate Recovery program two times before I yielded to the Holy Spirit and asked Him to help me be vulnerable and honest. Through the process, He began changing my distorted view of God, myself, and others. When the Enemy tried to dig up past hurts and false beliefs that made me limp by faith, the Holy Spirit pointed me to the victory Christ already won.

Of course my past affects me and the way I perceive and

approach life. However, my loving Father would never allow temporal things to distort my identity, determine my value, define my purpose, or destroy my future. I can ask the Holy Spirit to keep me from the sin of idolatry by revealing when I place anything or anyone above Him, including my past or my "self." While sojourning through this world, sustained by and surrendered to the Spirit of God, I can receive support from others without fear and serve others from a place of healing, holiness, and hope. With triumphant praises, I can sink into the trustworthy embrace of the one true God who loves me. He gave Himself for me, so I can rest in His presence and be past tense, present tense, and continually freed . . . forever.

When the apostle Paul encouraged the church in Colossae, he wrote, "Since, then, you have been raised with Christ, set your hearts on things above, where Christ is, seated at the right hand of God. Set your minds on things above, not on earthly things. For you died, and your life is now hidden with Christ in God" (Colossians 3:1–3). We serve a living God who already reigns because He never stopped being King. Jesus is returning, so we can walk in victory all the time and trust we will "appear with him in glory" (v. 4). Our hope in Christ fuels our peace, secures our freedom, and strengthens our resolve when conflicts arise or life pounds us with hardship.

Knowing the believers would struggle, Paul said, "Put to death, therefore, whatever belongs to your earthly nature" (v. 5). By the power of the Spirit, they could reject the comfort and complacency of living according to their fleshly desires. God had released them from the bondage of their old selves. So Paul told the disciples that they "*used* to walk in these ways," past tense, before they received Christ (v. 7). The disciples had all they needed to live in freedom because they were walking in the present and in the presence of God Himself.

By continually seeking to know God, they could be mindful of spiritual things and walk in alignment with Him. Paul said, "Do not lie to each other, since you have taken off your old self with its practices and have put on the new self, which is being renewed in knowledge in the image of its Creator" (vv. 9–10). Paul's statement inferred that believers were already changed and always changing. Due to the work Jesus had already done and the presence of the Spirit who already dwelled in them, the disciples would never have to revert to who they were in their before-Jesus days.

The ongoing tug-of-war between what was and what is, between flesh and spirit, is a real struggle. Inviting the Holy Spirit into the fight, bowing to His authority, and trusting that God keeps His word ends the battle. As Paul wrote in verse 12, "Therefore, as God's chosen people, holy and dearly loved, clothe yourselves with compassion, kindness, humility, gentleness and patience." This sweet fragrance of the fruit of the Spirit will always be evident in the abundant life flowing through one who is freed in Christ.

However, the apostle knew that even those who loved Jesus and were devoted to following Him would not always live like they are free in Christ. He gave the believers the key to unlock that freedom and cultivate that fruit. He said, "Let the message of Christ dwell among you richly as you teach and admonish one another with all wisdom through psalms, hymns, and songs from the Spirit, singing to God with gratitude in your hearts" (v. 16). Steadied by God's truth, which was prophesied in the Old Testament, the believers would stand together and grow together. Paul's final charge was a call to a life of community worship: "Whatever you do, whether in word or deed, do it all in the name of the Lord Jesus, giving thanks to God the Father through him"

(v. 17). This lifestyle of grateful worship encompasses every aspect of our being and doing.

A victorious life in Christ cannot be experienced while we are separated from the body of Christ. We are not self-sufficient. Even when we think we're doing something on our own, we are reliant on God. Scripture says "everything" belongs to God, even the "highest heavens" and the "earth and everything in it" (Deuteronomy 10:14). In Job 41:11, God Himself said, "Whatever is under the whole heaven is mine" (ESV). The writer of Hebrews declared, "The Son is the radiance of God's glory and the exact representation of his being, sustaining all things by his powerful word" (1:3). So, even those who reject God's love, who don't give Him credit as creator and sustainer of all, cannot physically live one second without all He provides.

We can stop trying to preserve ourselves, stop striving to maintain a false sense of security or control, stop waiting to cry out in desperation when we have no one to turn to *but* God. Placing God on the throne doesn't stifle us or make us prisoners stuck under the thumb of a power-hungry ruler with a dictator's heart. Submission to Christ, possible only through our surrender to the Spirit, enables us to encounter God intimately so He can heal us and make us holy. From that sacred and safe place of wholeness, He gives us all we need to do whatever He has planned for us. As we honor Him with each extraordinary ordinary moment He gives us, we are freed to live and love like Jesus—to be all he created us to be for our good and His glory.

Inhale

> Whatever you do, whether in word or deed, do it all in the name of the Lord Jesus, giving thanks to God the Father through him. (Colossians 3:17)

Exhale

Freedom-giving Spirit of God, thanks for revealing our sins, our trauma, and our false thinking in the safety of Your healing presence. Help us embrace our new lives in Christ. We are so grateful that neither our past sins nor the sins of those who sinned against us can enslave us, determine our value, or make us useless vessels. Empower us to confess, repent, seek forgiveness, and forgive others, so that nothing can keep us from living in holiness and loving from a place of wholeness. In Jesus's name, amen.

SACRED STRIDE

Ask the Holy Spirit to help you take an inventory of all the

- things you've done that hurt yourself, others, and God;
- things others have done to hurt you and God; and
- sins that still tempt you.

Then ask the Spirit to forgive you, help you forgive, and help you walk daily in your freedom through Christ our Lord.

30

Living for the King

STEP INTO GOD'S WORD
1 Peter 1:1–12

STAND ON GOD'S TRUTH
*The Holy Spirit strengthens our resolve and deepens
our commitment to kingdom advancement.*

James's dad served as a traveling pastor and church planter
in the Philippines, even when culture and logic told them
to go the opposite way. In 1987, while his parents were on the
road, James's ten-year-old sister drowned in a tragic accident.
As the family mourned, God gave James's father an opportunity
to serve as a missionary in the United States. Wanting to obey
God and provide a better life, he left his family to share the
gospel and plant churches in the United States.

Though the separation was hard, God reunited the family
in America five years later. But James's father was committed
to advancing God's kingdom, so they moved every three years
to serve wherever God led. As James grew older, however, he
struggled to maintain relationships with others and with God.

And when he started college, he entered the party scene and stopped attending church.

God did not stop pursuing James, though.

While James worked as a substitute teacher, he ran into a man who had served as his youth counselor during a middle school camp. Though James continued partying, he felt safe in Pastor Bill's church. He enjoyed their honest conversations. Their approach to ministry intrigued him. The church served the community even while playing kickball in the park. For the first time in James's life, he invited friends to church. Many of the people who joined him were not Christian.

During that time, James had no idea that his dad was praying for him.

On his way home from celebrating his twenty-first birthday with friends, James began to feel guilty. He started crying because he knew he was grieving the Spirit of God. The next day, his dad told James of his prayers for him. He mentioned that a youth camp needed counselors. James told his dad he couldn't help because he wasn't "good." But after a restless night wrestling with God, James agreed to serve at the camp.

After he arrived, God began healing James while using him to share the gospel with kids who were also looking for healing, hope, and purpose. James wanted to get away, but he didn't have a car. He tried to sneak out to a party, but his friends couldn't find him. As he sat by the bonfire one night, he asked God to help him fully surrender. When James returned home, he began sharing the gospel whenever God gave him an opportunity. James's parents saw the change in him. They told him they had been praying for him to be a pastor since the day he was born.

James did not want to be a pastor.

He did, however, start a Bible study.

James lost friends when he started following God, but he met Pia two years later. He felt the Holy Spirit nudging him toward full-time ministry before he married Pia in 2007. So when they started praying together, the Holy Spirit aligned their hearts with His. And in God's perfect timing, James ran into Pastor Bill again. James knew their meetings were divine appointments, not coincidences. Pastor Bill needed an associate pastor. And James was willing. After Pastor Bill helped him get his ordination, James served under his leadership for two years.

As God began growing their family, James went to seminary. After graduation, God opened the doors for them to plant a church in San Francisco. In 2014, as they praised God for the incredible ways He was providing, James's dad began cancer treatments. With confident and expectant faith, James prayed with his dad weekly and interceded for him daily. His dad lived for the advancement of God's kingdom and wanted to keep serving the Lord. James had witnessed God healing others. He believed God would have mercy and heal his dad. But in March 2017, his dad started saying goodbyes. While James grappled with his heavenly Father, his earthly father was excited to go home—and very soon, he did. James couldn't even cry.

During his dad's celebration-of-life ceremony, the Holy Spirit comforted James as he interacted with people from all over the world who had served God with his dad. The Spirit reminded James that Jesus is forever worthy of worship, devotion, and faithful service, even amid suffering and loss.

That same year, James, Pia, and their three sons followed God's leading and moved to Texas. And while adjusting to his new leadership position, after a year of mourning inwardly, James finally wept over the loss of his dad.

Five and a half years later, God opened the door to a senior pastorship at a multiethnic, multicultural, and multigenerational church in California. James's family moved back to the state, and James, like his dad, determined to rely on the Holy Spirit no matter what. Taking one sacred stride at a time, he devoted his life to God's kingdom movement.

God has always remained with His people through trials and affliction, deepening their faith while using them to serve others and expand His kingdom. The apostle Peter said believers "have been chosen according to the foreknowledge of God the Father, through the sanctifying work of the Spirit, to be obedient to Jesus Christ and sprinkled with his blood" (1 Peter 1:2). We have been handpicked by the Godhead to leave behind our worldly ways and receive a new life through Christ (v. 3). Our salvation is secure, an "inheritance that can never perish, spoil or fade" (v. 4). And God will shield us, His beloved children, even when we suffer "grief in all kinds of trials" (vv. 5–6).

Though believers aren't exempt from the hardships of life or from persecution as we share the gospel, God uses our afflictions to establish the authenticity of our faith. He deepens our commitment to Christ by bolstering our hope in Him, a process designed to "result in praise, glory and honor when Jesus Christ is revealed" (v. 7).

Once we accept Jesus as our Savior and Lord, the Spirit empowers us to live with bold faith no matter how weak or discouraged we may feel. "Though you have not seen [Jesus], you love him," Peter wrote, "and even though you do not see him now, you believe in him and are filled with an inexpressible and glorious joy, for you are receiving the end result of your faith, the salvation of your souls" (vv. 8–9).

The apostle drew upon the trustworthy Old Testament prophets, God's proven spokesmen, who prophesied the coming, suffering, and victory of the Messiah (vv. 10–12). God's people coming after them could look to Jesus and recognize the fulfillment of the Scriptures.

With our fidelity and joy built on the unshakable foundation of Scripture, from Genesis through Revelation, we can walk "with minds that are alert and fully sober" as we set our hope on Jesus, who will return again (v. 13). God the Spirit enables us to live as "obedient children," who "do not conform to the evil desires" we bowed down to when we "lived in ignorance" (v. 14). With an eternal perspective, we can live as grateful victors set apart to serve the King of Kings.

"Just as he who called you is holy, so be holy in all you do," Peter continued, "for it is written: 'Be holy, because I am holy'" (vv. 15–16). Holiness is mandatory if we are to serve as Christ's ambassadors. But we can't fix ourselves by striving to be good enough for God to use. The Holy Spirit alone can make us holy by living in us as He helps us live in Him. He is the one who sets us apart, prepping us for the pruning shears, the refining fires, the soul sifting that makes us more like Jesus each day.

As foreigners on earth, God's people will endure suffering. However, we can trust that God protects us, provides for us, and molds our character so we reflect the heart of Christ *while* He transforms us and uses us for His glory. We can rely on the Spirit's unlimited power and grace. The one true God will strengthen our resolve and enable us to remain committed to His kingdom movement.

Inhale

> With minds that are alert and fully sober, set your hope on the grace to be brought to you when Jesus Christ is revealed at his coming. (1 Peter 1:13)

Exhale

Life-changing Spirit of God, thanks for pursuing us when we fail to pursue You. Give us eyes to see those who feel invisible or insignificant. Give us ears to hear those who feel unheard or misunderstood. Give us hearts to love those who feel unworthy or unprotected. Help us trust You when we are the ones who need to be reminded that we're seen, heard, and loved. Please carry us through trials, strengthen us, and increase our faith as You give us opportunities to share the good news and love the people You place in our path. Help us want to know You, serve You, commit to Your kingdom movement, and live in a way that makes others want to do the same. In Jesus's name, amen.

SACRED STRIDE

Ask the Holy Spirit to show you how He wants you to use your God-given talents, treasures, and time as He empowers you to remain intentional and committed to expanding God's kingdom.

31

Flourishing Fruit

STEP INTO GOD'S WORD
Galatians 5:13–26

STAND ON GOD'S TRUTH
The Holy Spirit makes His fruit flourish as we follow Him.

A year after we moved to Wisconsin, I began planning to promote my first devotional, *Waiting for God: Trusting Him for the Answers to Every Prayer*. I had no local friends to help. Succumbing to a pity party, I begged God to take me back home to California.

Later that day, my editor invited me to speak at chapel and sign books at the Our Daily Bread Ministries offices in Grand Rapids, Michigan. As I praised God, He reminded me of all the good things He'd done since my family had arrived in the Midwest. I asked Him to forgive me for being ungrateful and to help me trust His leading. And I thanked Him for the blessings and the struggles that proved His mighty, merciful presence. That's when I started seeing His fingerprints of faithfulness in unexpected places.

Before our move, God had given me peace about it even

though I didn't want to leave our sons. Then after our relocation, He used a fellow writer to introduce me to Carmen, my first friend in Fond du Lac. It was Carmen who helped us adopt my service dog, Callie, from a kill shelter. And from there, one thing led to another.

While walking my new puppy one day, an older couple who lived by the park offered their porch as a rest stop. Jan and Dave—whom we came to call Grandma and Grandpa—proved to be my biggest ministry supporters in the Midwest.

Alan's colleague, Superbowl champion Green Bay Packers' linebacker Dr. George Koonce, and his wife, Gina, made us feel seen, understood, and at home as we adjusted to life in the Midwest. Gina introduced us to ReachOut Bookstore & Solid Grounds Coffee Shoppe. Their staff prayed for us as we searched for a church. The owners of ReachOut helped raise funds for Sol's service dog to be trained through Tails for Life. They even hosted the launch party for my first children's picture book, *Different Like Me*, in August 2020.

My search for medical help with my debilitating pain found its answer when God led me to my praying doctor. He helped me find the first medicine that managed the stabbing pain in my thoracic spine since my injury in 1992. His wife, Patty, became my friend and prayer partner until Jesus unexpectedly called her home.

The kind staff at our veterinary clinic supported us when we had to say goodbye to Jazzy, our sixteen-year-old miracle mutt. They also introduced us to Jake and Amanda, the owners of Tails for Life, whom you met in chapter 18.

When I began longing for deeper connections, our neighbors Rick and Rita were the first people to invite us into their home. They turned on a light in their living room while praying and reading the Bible. I could look from my window late at night and see that beacon of hope shining, reminding me that Alan and I were not alone, even before God finally led us to a church family.

I couldn't even list all the names of the people God used to bless us in Fond du Lac—the people I pray felt blessed by us. As I praised God for them, it dawned on me that I had to repent. I had been so busy wanting to leave that I failed to appreciate what God was doing right in front of me.

Preoccupied with discontent, I failed to rest in God's presence and recognize His blessings in the present. I asked for His forgiveness and thanked Him for affirming that I am always home because He is always with me. I also thanked Him for reminding me that He worked through my times of suffering, often in ways that would never be possible apart from that suffering.

In September 2020, God moved us back to California unexpectedly. We had twenty-eight days to pack up, move across the country, and find a place to live before Alan started his new job. Though thrilled to leave the Wisconsin weather, I grieved leaving the neighbors I'd grown to love. I cried in front of Grandma Jan's house when Amanda and her daughter, Kinslee, came to say goodbye. And I cried when we prayed with Rick and Rita before leaving for the airport.

Once back in California, I was so happy to be home and close to my sons. But life did not get easier. I immediately asked God to make me more aware of His presence and more grateful for the wonderful things He was doing, even when our circumstances didn't feel wonderful.

We had to stay in a hotel for a month until we found an apartment. The church we had attended since 2008 no longer had a senior pastor, so I joined the search committee. Unable to drive and yearning for fellowship, I prayed for my neighbors while walking Callie around our apartment complex. During one of those walks I met Shari, a lover of Jesus who wanted to start a weekly Bible study.

After my lower spine damage led to a one-week hospital stay, our realtor and *comadre*, Cynthia, begged God to lead her to a house that would end our two-year search in a competitive seller's market. The Holy Spirit used a wrong turn to lead her to a new development. As we talked about prayer and how good God had been to us with the realtor in charge of the development, she mentioned a two-story house with a downstairs office, a huge yard, and a selling price *under* our budget. We would be first on the list if we were interested. We submitted the paperwork, drove to *our* corner lot, stood in the middle of the dirt, and worshiped God. We moved in March of 2022 as Alan was healing from surgery on his Achilles' heel. Then in 2023, good news for our church: a new senior pastor and his family stepped into leadership.

While my husband recovered from six surgeries between 2022 and 2024, multiple health setbacks of my own caused me increased pain and fatigue. On many days I couldn't even get out of bed. I struggled with debilitating headaches, nerve pain, and spasms. But the Holy Spirit motivated and strengthened me as I continued writing for the *Our Daily Bread* devotional and the *God Hears Her* blog and worked to complete this book. And God sent others to encourage me and pray with me.

He also blessed me with the pleasure and privilege of contributing the "Choose to Change" feature in *The Go Bible for Kids*, which released in 2024 and was an answer to a prayer I mumbled in 2001. I prayed and wept as I finished two more picture books I started writing in 2019, *What Color is God's Love?* and *Wonderfully, Marvelously Brown*. Both released in 2024. All these projects were inspired by heartbreaking personal experiences that God transformed to hope-filled testimonies, and only completed as He enabled me to type one sacred word at a time.

Whether the roads were smooth, twisted, rocky, washed out, or leading to a dead end, God remained with me. He interwove the lives of His people with Alan's and mine to fulfill His purposes for us. When I stopped desiring comfort over closeness with God, the Holy Spirit helped me recognize the flagstone blessings on the path He had preordained for my good and His glory. And when I asked for His leading and followed Him in His power, His fruit flourished in my life and through my relationships.

In a letter to the Galatians, the apostle Paul reminded them that believers in Jesus "were called to be free" and warned them not to use their freedom "to indulge the flesh," but to "serve one another humbly in love" (Galatians 5:13). Paul said that "the entire law is fulfilled in keeping this one command: 'Love your neighbor as yourself'" (v. 14). He pointed to the importance of the believers' personal relationships with God and one another, individually and as a community.

Paul didn't separate the characteristics we know as the fruit of the Spirit, because these characteristics are not nurtured apart from one another or the ways we serve each other. He said that "the *fruit* of the Spirit is love, joy, peace, forbearance, kindness, goodness, faithfulness, gentleness and self-control" (vv. 22–23, emphasis mine). He then affirmed our God-given and God-empowered commission: "Since we live by the Spirit, let us keep in step with the Spirit" (v. 25). To keep in step means to follow faithfully, which is impossible without knowing God's Word and praying.

After Jesus taught the disciples how to pray in Luke 11:1–4, He emphasized the importance of persistent prayer (vv. 5–10). He explained to them how a loving father would provide when asked by his child, then brought it home: "If you then, though you are evil, know how to give good gifts to your children, how much more will your Father in heaven give the Holy Spirit to those who ask him!" (vv. 11–13). Jesus was revealing the importance of asking for the Holy Spirit, receiving Him, acknowledging His constant presence, and accessing His power by praying continually (1 Thessalonians 5:17).

When we pray with each sacred stride we take, the Holy Spirit endows us with everything we need to walk in His presence and power. As He cultivates His fruit through stillness and storms, our reliance on Him remains crucial and rewarding. We will experience growing pains as the Spirit prunes our character so that His fruit will flourish in and through our lives.

As we surrender with all our hearts, the Holy Spirit enables us to love our neighbors with acts of kindness, gentleness, and goodness. He won't just give us peace—He becomes our peace as He equips us to practice forbearance, or patience, with faithfulness and self-control when we interact with Him and others. Though we will fail, sometimes miserably, the Holy Spirit will never fail us. In His strength we can place Him first. As we seek Him, submit to Him, and follow Him, God the Spirit will make His fruit flourish and make our lives and our relationships fragrant with the scent of Christ's love.

Inhale

> Since we live by the Spirit, let us keep in step with the Spirit. (Galatians 5:25)

Exhale

Sanctifying Spirit of God, thanks for reminding us that we're at home wherever we are and amid whatever is going on around us, simply because You are with us. Forgive us for the times we desire comfort over closeness with You. Please empower us to yield to You and trust You're always working for the good of all who love You. That means life is not just about us. We are ready and willing to have You prune away our thorns and make Your fruit flourish as we submit to You one sacred stride at a time. In Jesus's name, amen.

SACRED STRIDE

Ask the Holy Spirit to help you to acknowledge Him continually as He cultivates His fruit in your life. Trust Him to provide all you need to love Him and your beautifully diverse neighbors with your attitudes, actions, and your words.

Conclusion
Where Do I Go from Here?

STEP INTO GOD'S WORD
Psalm 139:1–18

STAND ON GOD'S TRUTH
The Holy Spirit is already and always with us, wherever we go.

A friend called me when she was supposed to be at work and said that she felt like running away. I invited her to come over. During our conversation, she confessed that she wouldn't even mind if God took her home. I told her I had said similar words a few years prior and had shared that story in the first chapter of *Waiting for God*. I prayed for the words my friend needed. Instead, the Holy Spirit gave me the words *we* needed.

She had been the person God used to help me find a church when I returned home after a three-month separation from my husband. I knew Jesus was her Savior and the Holy Spirit dwelled in her. I reminded her that we don't have to be or even feel strong enough because He was always enough. Relief showed tangibly on her face when I told her the saying "God won't give you more than you can handle" was a false, unbiblical teaching. She shared how she had been struggling because she believed that phrase since childhood. When she in fact *couldn't* handle her situation, she didn't know what to do.

I assured my friend we could trust Jesus because He is "the image of the invisible God, the firstborn over all creation. For in him all things were created: things in heaven and on earth, visible and invisible, whether thrones or powers or rulers or authorities; all things have been created through him and for him. He is before all things, and in him all things hold together" (Colossians 1:15–17). Everything revolves around Jesus, God the Son.

The Holy Spirit brought a Bible story to my mind. Once again Moses was involved. This time, though, the holy ground he stood on wasn't in front of a burning bush. He was in the presence of Jesus.

Then I shared the story from Mark 9:1–13, where Peter, James, and John saw Jesus transfigured. "And there appeared before them Elijah and Moses, who were talking with Jesus" (v. 4). Elijah and Moses could talk to Jesus because in eternity they knew Him and connected with Him face-to-face. This moment can comfort us when our world falls apart because it proves Jesus is not just a great teacher, a prophet, or a good man. He is God, "the same yesterday and today and forever" (Hebrews 13:8).

The disciples saw Elijah and Moses disappear and heard God the Father give authority to the Son. But Jesus told them not to tell anyone "until the Son of Man had risen from the dead," and they had no idea what He meant at the time (Mark 9:9–10). God had prophesied through judges and prophets. The apostles were familiar with the Scriptures—what we now know as the Old Testament—which pointed to Jesus hundreds of years before He was born. But they could not understand without the illumination of the Holy Spirit.

After the transfiguration, the three returned with Jesus to a large crowd surrounding the other disciples, who were arguing with the teachers of the law (v. 14). A man whose son had been possessed by a spirit said the disciples were unable to drive it out. Jesus called the crowd an "unbelieving generation" and told the father to bring the boy to Him (vv. 17–19).

Jesus asked the father to explain his situation. This is the most intimate form of prayer: an honest conversation with Jesus that demonstrates our trust that He hears and helps us. However, after the father told Jesus what had been going on since the boy was a child, he said, "If you can do anything, take pity on us and help us" (v. 22). He had brought his son to Jesus, but somewhere deep inside, the heartbroken father still doubted.

> "'If you can'?" said Jesus. "Everything is possible for one who believes."
> Immediately the boy's father exclaimed, "I do believe; help me overcome my unbelief!" (vv. 23–24)

The man's response was a humble prayer admitting his limitations. God alone could fill the gaps in his faith. And only God can supply what we ourselves need to live a life of faith.

Jesus commanded the spirit to leave the boy and never return. The boy convulsed as the spirit immediately obeyed Jesus and left the boy "like a corpse. . . . But Jesus took him by the hand and lifted him to his feet" (vv. 25–27). Later in private, when the disciples asked why their own attempt to drive out the spirit hadn't succeeded, Jesus said, "This kind can come out only by prayer" (v. 29).

Recently Jesus had sent the disciples on a mission with authority to heal and cast out demons (Mark 6:7–13). They returned with a glowing report. They had experienced amazing success—but now, failure. What had gone wrong? What were they missing? Apparently not all situations were the same. And as Jesus's words implied, all demons weren't the same either.

So what would make the difference? One thing: prayer, the relational link to God and His guidance and power.

For the woman with the issue of blood in Mark 5:25–34, reaching out to touch Jesus's robe was her prayer. Desperation led her to act, but she acted in faith. She believed Jesus could heal her. Once healed, she risked everything to come forward and testify of His power. And Jesus, in response, called her "daughter," affirming that she was known, seen, heard, accepted, and loved.

During Jesus's three-year earthly ministry, the disciples remained close to Him and listened to His teaching. He taught them how to pray, both by word and by example. They saw Him slip away often to be with the Father. Jesus modeled to His disciples a life of prayer, dependent on intimate relationship with and surrender to His Father.

In the garden of Gethsemane, Jesus showed us how to yield in prayer: "'*Abba*, Father,' he said, 'everything is possible for you. Take this cup from me. Yet not what I will, but what you will'" (Mark 14:36). He remained connected with the Father and the Spirit as a member of the Godhead, except for the moment He took our sins upon Him on the cross (Mark 15:34).

The instant we place our trust in Jesus as our Savior, we receive the same Holy Spirit. Yet many of us do not walk in His constant power and presence or submit to Jesus as Lord. We settle for self-empowered rather than Spirit-empowered faith when we fail to depend on Jesus as the author who initiates our faith and the perfecter who completes it (Hebrews 12:2).

Before my friend left that day, we prayed, "Help us overcome our unbelief."

The tension between belief and unbelief is a blurred line of desperation, often undetectable until we've run out of options. But we are always out of options without God. We are all physically, mentally, emotionally, and spiritually depleted any time we are not abiding in Christ, connecting with Him, relying on the Spirit of God. We struggle to "pray continually" because we forget that the Holy Spirit intercedes for us (1 Thessalonians 5:16–18; Romans 8:26–27). Jesus Himself prayed for us yesterday and continues praying for us today and forever (John 17:1–26; Romans 8:34; Hebrews 7:23–28). And we can pray in the Spirit as we pray for each other (Ephesians 6:18).

Believers don't have to beg the Holy Spirit to come because He is already in us. Through the presence of the Spirit, the true, triune God is always with us. He knows us, sees us, hears us, and loves us. He accepts us, transforms us, redeems us, and more, so much more. This is the God we serve. So we can inhale—take in, ponder, and believe—the unchanging and life-changing truth in Psalm 139.

Inhale

> You have searched me, LORD,
> and you know me.
> You know when I sit and when I rise;
> you perceive my thoughts from afar.
> You discern my going out and my lying down;
> you are familiar with all my ways.
> Before a word is on my tongue
> you, LORD, know it completely.
> You hem me in behind and before,
> and you lay your hand upon me.
> Such knowledge is too wonderful for me,
> too lofty for me to attain.
>
> Where can I go from your Spirit?
> Where can I flee from your presence?

If I go up to the heavens, you are there;
    if I make my bed in the depths, you are there.
If I rise on the wings of the dawn,
    if I settle on the far side of the sea,
even there your hand will guide me,
    your right hand will hold me fast.
If I say, "Surely the darkness will hide me
    and the light become night around me,"
even the darkness will not be dark to you;
    the night will shine like the day,
    for darkness is as light to you.

For you created my inmost being;
    you knit me together in my mother's womb.
I praise you because I am fearfully and
        wonderfully made;
    your works are wonderful,
    I know that full well.
My frame was not hidden from you
    when I was made in the secret place,
    when I was woven together in the depths of
        the earth.
Your eyes saw my unformed body;
    all the days ordained for me were written in
        your book
    before one of them came to be.
How precious to me are your thoughts, God!
    How vast is the sum of them!
Were I to count them,
    they would outnumber the grains of sand—
    when I awake, I am still with you.
(Psalm 139:1–18)

Exhale

To God be the glory, the honor, and the praise! Amen.

So, where do we go from here?

There is only one more sacred stride to take as we thank God for *being* "our refuge and strength, an ever-present help in trouble" (Psalm 46:1).

SACRED STRIDE

Ask the Holy Spirit to help you live with a constant awareness of His presence in the present, and pray:

> *Holy Spirit, I am ready. I am willing. I am Yours.*
> *Do what You will. Hallelujah!*

My Prayer for You

I pray that out of his glorious riches he may strengthen you with power through his Spirit in your inner being, so that Christ may dwell in your hearts through faith. And I pray that you, being rooted and established in love, may have power, together with all the Lord's holy people, to grasp how wide and long and high and deep is the love of Christ, and to know this love that surpasses knowledge—that you may be filled to the measure of all the fullness of God (Ephesians 3:16–19).
> *In Jesus's name, amen.*

GOD HEARS HER.

Seek and she will find

Spread the Word
by Doing One Thing.

- Give a copy of this book as a gift.
- Share the QR code link via your social media.
- Write a review of this book on your blog, favorite bookseller's website, or at ourdailybreadpublishing.org.
- Recommend this book to your church, small group, or book club.

Connect with us. 🅕 🅞

Our Daily Bread Publishing
PO Box 3566, Grand Rapids, MI 49501, USA
Email: books@odbm.org

Love God. Love Others.

with  Our Daily Bread.

Your gift changes lives.

Connect with us. 🅕 ⓘ

Our Daily Bread Publishing
PO Box 3566, Grand Rapids, MI 49501, USA
Email: books@odbm.org